INTERPRETIVE
writing

Alan Leftridge

P.O. Box 2246
Fort Collins, CO 80522

NAI is a private nonprofit [501(c)3] organization and
professional association. NAI's mission is: "Inspiring
leadership and excellence to advance heritage
interpretation as a profession." For information, visit
www.interpnet.com.

ISBN 1–879931–21–4

For my parents

Lorraine Leftridge and
Leonard Leftridge

CONTENTS

FOREWORD

I am often reminded of the old saying, "If a tree falls in the forest and no one is there to hear it, does it make a sound?" Interpretive writers also have a saying: "If an agency puts a sign in a forest and no one bothers to read it, does it make any difference?" In my view, the answer to the second question is obvious. Of course it makes a difference—to the agency that spent its money unwisely. It doesn't, however, make any difference to the audience for whom it was intended because the message was never delivered.

Therein lies the inherent problem with interpretive writing. Much of the work I performed as a consultant over 30 years involved writing or editing text for interpretive exhibits, signs, and publications. Although I enjoyed the creative process of writing and the challenge of crafting text with a message (as opposed to simply writing descriptions), I often had a difficult time convincing the "ologists" associated with interpretive projects that the audience might have a difficult time connecting with scientific terminology or complex concepts that only a fellow Ph.D. in the subject area would be able to grasp. Fascinating subjects, frustrating process.

I realized the resource experts knew their stuff far better than I ever would. I also realized that they did not fully understand the definition or purpose of interpretation. When left to write text for signs or exhibits, they had a tendency to go overboard with data, using the "book on a stick" approach—and they'd see nothing wrong with that. After all, most people learn to write a sentence in third grade, so it should be easy to write interpretive text, right? I can pick up a paintbrush and apply it to a canvas also, but that doesn't necessarily make me an artist.

Interpretive writing is a specialized skill. It is not journalism, or creative writing, or technical writing. It is, perhaps, one of the most powerful types of writing that can be employed because when done well enough that people read it, a message is delivered. The National Association for Interpretation defines interpretation as a communication process that forges emotional and intellectual connections between the interests of the audience and the meanings inherent in the resource. Interpretive writing, then, is one of the communication processes by which those connections are made. It follows interpretive principles, including "audience-appropriateness."

I applaud Alan's efforts in training good writers to become good interpretive writers. This long-overdue book provides excellent guidance to those who must write interpretive text, regardless of their current skill level. Gentle reminders for those with experience blend with important tips for beginners. I look forward to seeing continuing improvement in interpretive text everywhere as a result.

Lisa Brochu
NAI Associate Director
September, 2006

PREFACE

The purpose of this book is to share some of the things I have learned as an interpretive writer. Since 1976, I have written a variety of brochures, panels, and articles, edited newsletters, edited The Western Interpreters Association's *The Interpreter* magazine, and edited the National Association for Interpretation's *Legacy* and *The Interpreter* magazines. In 2002, I started conducting the "Art of Interpretive Writing" workshops all over the United States. More than 1,000 participants have attended. My instructing, writing, and editing experiences have convinced me that interpretive writing for natural history and cultural heritage subjects is an exclusive style. As a genre, its elements are identifiable and measurable.

Because interpretive writing is a genre, quantifiable assessment forms can measure the degree to which a writing sample is interpretive. Therefore, the second purpose of this book is to provide a framework for evaluating interpretive writing and to present a review of effective interpretive writing practices.

Finally, the third purpose of this book is to share a process for writing interpretive messages. This process is similar to ones followed by other writing styles but has variations that are exclusive to interpretive writing.

My academic background is in biology, education, and earth science, with formal training as a seasonal interpreter in Yellowstone National Park. I am not a trained journalist or university writing instructor. I am certain that some of my high school and college English teachers would scoff if they knew I were authoring a book about writing. Nevertheless, it is important to remember that much of what we learn is outside a formal education setting and comes from experience. My experiences include spending innumerable hours alone writing, and uncountable conversations with people who write about natural and cultural heritage subjects. I like telling people this because three out of four participants in my "Art of Interpretive Writing" workshops express anxiety about writing. Many of them are interpreters trained in the processes of verbal communication and have been assigned by their supervisor to write texts. Others have begun writing texts because they want to master another communication form. Neither group has a formal writing background in English or journalism. They are more likely trained historians, educators, or resource specialists.

Hearing that my formal training is in the sciences relieves some of the anxiety of workshop participants. I try to dispel more anxiety by quoting a friend, Catherine Arnold, who said, "Writing can be fun, but it is not easy. Anyone who says it is easy is not as good a writer as they think." Finally, I tell the participants that I find writing very difficult. I encourage them by reminding them that I have learned to write interpretive texts, and they can learn as well.

The story of my preparation for writing this book begins in 1980. At that time, I was teaching interpretation and environmental education courses at Humboldt State University in California. That autumn, I attended a Western Interpreters Association (WIA) meeting in Chico, California, along with several of my students. Three of the students approached me after a session in which President Hal Hallett announced that the editor of the association's magazine had resigned. The association was looking for a new editor and the students volunteered me.

My previous formal experience with print media was editing a periodic newsletter known as the *PWEEP Perennial*. I was the editor for two years while teaching at Miami University. The *Perennial* was a 12-page newsletter sent to alumni and students. It was not a magazine with photographs, numerous authors, and a circulation of over a thousand; WIA's magazine was.

I laughed and told my students to stop volunteering me for assignments. They continued to press their various points and finally persuaded me to accept the editorship. The best part of their persuasion was that I would review dozens of article submissions from all over the country and would be able to address issues raised in the articles in my classes long before the articles got into print. The students framed their position as a professional development issue. Finally, with big smiles, they said they would help by serving on the editorial board and being graphic designers. Their promises, smiles, and perseverance convinced me. I agreed, went to the officers of the Western Interpreters Association, and volunteered to be the new editor of *The Interpreter* magazine. The only thing I had not foreseen was that the students would graduate and leave me with the magazine to produce.

My tenure as editor of WIA's *The Interpreter* magazine lasted six years. As my student designers/editorial assistants graduated, others took their places. I always had plenty of help. My editorship ended when I accepted a one-year leave of absence from the university to teach on the island of Guam. Capable people edited the magazine in my absence. When I returned to California a year later, the Western Interpreters Association would join with the Association of Interpretive Naturalists to become the National Association for Interpretation. WIA's *The Interpreter* magazine was retired; NAI's *Journal of Interpretation* absorbed it.

In late May of 1989, I got a telephone call from NAI's vice president for programs, Ron Russo. He told me that the editor of *The Journal of Interpretation* resigned and wanted to know if I would take the position. This time, I needed no persuasion. I liked editing magazines. I accepted the opportunity to learn more about interpretation by editing the journal. At the end of 1990, the journal's name changed to *Legacy* magazine. I remained editor of *Legacy* for the next 14 years.

The role of *Legacy* in its early years was to provide communication from the national office to members and have articles of broad interest to interpreters. Many issues of *Legacy* had time-sensitive news, as well as feature articles, commentary pieces, and research manuscripts. The magazine changed year-by-year, in part, because NAI began publishing *The Journal of Interpretation Research* and *InterpNews*. Publishing the journal removed research-related material from *Legacy; InterpNews* absorbed time-sensitive material from Legacy. This meant that the articles appearing in *Legacy* were more specific to the interests of front-line interpreters, planners, and managers. That too, was going to change.

Inspired by an idea expressed at the 1996 National Interpreters Workshop in Billings, Montana, *Legacy* was going to change into a publication that would broadcast the role of interpretation in society to a much larger audience. In the category of *Natural History, Smithsonian*, and *National Geographic* magazines, *Legacy* would serve the profession as an outreach publication, informing the public about the purpose of interpretation. The move toward fulfilling this vision began in earnest in 2004. My role in the process was to leave *Legacy* magazine and edit a new publication directed at practicing front-line interpreters, managers, and planners, with the new magazine named *The Interpreter*.

Several months before the 2002 National Interpreters Workshop in Virginia Beach, Virginia, NAI Associate Director Lisa Brochu invited me to conduct a two-day pre-workshop session on interpretive writing. I asked, "Why me?" She reminded me that since 1980 I had read hundreds of articles that appeared—and did not appear—in both *The Interpreter* and *Legacy*. Consequently, I would have an understanding about what makes good interpretive writing. That workshop was more successful than I expected, signaling a need that interpreters have for writing experiences. This encouraged me to continue conducting interpretive writing workshops. Since 2002, I have conducted more than 85 "Art of Interpretive Writing" workshops around the United States. I chose to include the word *art* in the title of the workshop because I believe that writing is an art form. Just as an oil painter selects colors from his pallet to express a vision, interpretive writers select words, phrases, and cadences to tell a story.

The workshops have allowed me to work with hundreds of professional and amateur writers. Most of the participants are from government agencies (National Park Service, National Forest Service, Bureau of Land Management, Bureau of Reclamation, US Army Corps of Engineers, and various state and regional park departments). Writers and designers from zoos, arboretums, nature centers, and museums make up another group. Book authors, magazine editors, college writing instructors, and private contractors make up the final group of participants. I have learned a lot about writing and the writing process by interacting with all of these groups. Their varied perspectives have helped me galvanize my belief that interpretive writing is a specific genre.

There are those among you who will accept my assertion that interpretive writing is a genre without question. There are those among you who are skeptical and say, "Convince me." Others will say that interpretive writing is not an identifiable, quantifiable genre, but is just good writing. I assert that interpretive writing is more than good writing; it is an art form. You may ask, "How can you measure art?" It is possible to measure art; there are standards, a definable vocabulary, and specific criteria toward a purpose. Interpretive writing, too, has its definable elements. The reason for writing this book is to convince you of that fact.

PART ONE

the basics

BACKGROUND

Several people have made natural and cultural heritage interpretation their passion and have addressed interpretive writing in their books. Among the contributors to the field are Freeman Tilden, regarded by many as the father of interpretation, Ted Cable, Larry Beck, Sam Ham, Tim Merriman, Lisa Brochu, Beverly Serrell, and David Larsen. As interpreters, there is commonality among their perspectives. I feel it is important to review their perspectives to get a richer understanding of interpretive writing.

Freeman Tilden wrote *Interpreting Our Heritage* with front-line interpreters in mind. His discussion of interpretive writing appears in a chapter called "The Written Word" and reflects his experience as a playwright. The framework of the chapter is on three qualities of writing that should be applied to crafting interpretive signs, markers, labels, or printed literature: thinking, composition, and humor. Of the three, Tilden guessed, "that the adequate interpretive inscription will be the result of ninety percent thinking and ten percent composition."

Thinking permeates the writing process, whether you are creating ideas, researching, organizing your work, writing the first draft, rewriting, or revising. My experience is that I spend most of my time thinking about the subject I am going to write about, whether I am driving in my car, cutting firewood, recreating, listening to the radio, or doing the dishes. This serves as processing time in which I decide what the reader wants to read, think about what my client needs to express, formulate ideas how to best meet the needs of the reader and my client, and begin to craft phrases and sentences that will maintain the reader's attention. My processing time may take several days to several months. I consider this earnest work. During this time, I keep notes on ideas as they occur, often writing them on slips of paper I keep in my car and kitchen.

Thinking and processing time helps formulate how the finished composition will appear. Author Stephen King points out, "Writing is refined thinking." I believe that Freeman Tilden would have agreed.

Tilden also stressed brevity in composition. "The chief thing that makes the wording of good inscriptions so exacting is the requirement of brevity." Many interpretive messages are long because the writers do not focus on what the reader wants to read. Instead, the writer focuses on what they want the reader to know. Most writers know far more about the subject being interpreted than should appear in an interpretive piece. "What's worth knowing?" is a question every interpretive writer should ask before sitting down at his or her word processor. Texts are frequently too long because the writer does not ask this question or because the writer does not allow enough time to hone the piece. Mark Twain, in writing to an acquaintance, apologized for the letter's length: "I would have written a shorter letter if I had the time." Brevity is critical because most readers will lose focus if they are not enticed to continue. Tilden suggests that a way of luring readers on is by the "light touch."

As a playwright, Tilden was aware of the power of true humor to enchant audiences. It makes the story more human. Tilden referred to humor as the light touch rather than jokes, wit, or levity. Tilden concludes his chapter on writing noting, "When you are able to write with a light touch, without indulging in humor, then you shall be permitted to write humor with a light touch."

As pointed out by Dr. Larry Beck and Dr. Ted Cable in their book *Interpretation for the 21st Century*, "…Tilden did consider the mission and complexities of interpretive writing," but he "…said little about brochures, newsletters, feature articles, or correspondence that make up so much of interpreters' writing efforts today."

Beck and Cable discuss Tilden's three qualities of interpretive writing from modern perspectives in a chapter titled "Interpretive Composition." They also consider the conflicting views of using quotations in interpretive messages. Tilden did not discuss this at length, but in referring to the impact of a quotation at the Minuteman marker at Lexington Green, says, "Sometimes a quotation will be found more effective than anything we can currently invent." Beck and Cable conclude, "We encourage interpreters to use quotes to create a mood, stimulate reflection on the origin of the words, or stop readers in their tracks with a profound idea that came from someone else." Beck and Cable outline 15 guiding principles for interpreting nature and culture. One of the principles that relates to interpretive writing states: "Interpretive writing should address what readers would like to know, with the authority of wisdom and the humility and care that comes with it."

In *Environmental Interpretation*, Dr. Sam Ham presents 15 steps toward powerful exhibit texts. Among the steps, Ham cites research findings that stress writing thematically, using personal referencing, and keeping texts short. Although written for exhibit text preparation, the 15 steps provide guidelines that apply to most writing genres.

Addressing the whole and striving for message unity are covered in Beverly Serrell's *Exhibit Labels: An Interpretive Approach*. Serrell's book centers on the design elements of interpretive labels written for museums and zoos. The range of topics includes assessing audience characteristics, evaluation, and tasking. However, she begins the book with a discussion of crafting the "Big Idea" (wholeness and message unity). She asserts that labels must relate to a big idea, that the writing must provoke the reader, and the writing must address prior knowledge.

Lisa Brochu and Dr. Tim Merriman, in their book *Personal Interpretation*, discuss David Larsen's contributions to interpretive training in the National Park Service and United States Fish and Wildlife Service. Brochu and Merriman point out that Larsen has championed the approach of connecting the tangible attributes of the resource to the intangible meanings of the same. Larsen, an author of Module 101 of the National Park Service Interpretive Development Program, goes on to say that using a universal idea, a concept in which everyone has some understanding, facilitates the tangible-intangible connection.

Finally, in their book, *Signs, Trails, and Wayside Exhibits: Connecting People and Places*, part of the Interpreter's Handbook series, Suzanne Trapp, Michael Gross, and Ron Zimmerman identify seven ways to having an effective message. Three of the ways are design-related. The other four strategies are important to writers of all varieties, not just interpretive writers: keep it short, use action verbs, relate to the reader's experiences, and use metaphors, analogies, quotes, and real examples.

Several authors have provided directions for effectively communicating interpretive messages, whether front-line or non-personal. Their collective contributions illustrate that interpretive writing has many facets: that it is thematic, relevant, organized, entertaining, purposeful, it uses quotations, and addresses what the reader wants to know.

TYPES OF WRITING

There are many types of writing, none of which is mutually exclusive from the others. Overlapping exists. A partial list of styles includes scientific writing, science writing, historical writing, technical writing, promotional writing, journalism, informational writing, creative writing, medical writing, historical fiction, and propaganda—a manifestation of promotional writing.

One purpose of this book is to promote interpretive writing as a genre. Like other genres, interpretive writing is not exclusive of other styles. However, it has identifiable elements that set it apart. Two aspects that differentiate interpretive writing are that it is intended to make intellectual and emotional connections between the reader and the resource, and that it is goal-directed, with the intent of eliciting a pro-social response from readers. Definitions of the styles of writing that overlap interpretive writing are as follows:

Scientific writing is a form of writing that shares knowledge with groups that have similar academic backgrounds. This type of writing is based on fact and deduction and relies on technical scientific language. Scientific writing reports research findings, poses questions related to theories, and proposes hypotheses.

Science writing is based on fact and deduction, yet does not rely on technical scientific language. Science writing includes a human element, usually in first person in the form of a story. It answers the question, "What does this science concept or fact mean to me?" but does not elicit a pro-social response.

Historical writing is similar to scientific writing. This genre is used to communicate with readers who seek facts about past events.

Technical writing leads the reader to accomplish a specific task or learn a skill. It has its foundation in statistics, operations, and mechanical processes. It shares a basic principle with journalism: that the reader knows little about the subject. *Contrary to technical writing, interpretive writing builds upon the reader's prior knowledge.*

Promotional writing advances a product, cause, or organization. Manifestations of promotional writing include advertising, propaganda, public service announcements, and marketing.

Journalism includes news reports and related articles for media. Basic tenets of journalism include answering who, what, where, and when. The genre assumes that the readers have little prior knowledge of the subjects. *Like journalism, interpretive writing does not manipulate, it provides a balance and gives readers the right to draw their own conclusions.*

Informational writing includes factual data for reference or another use. Informational writing is often confused as interpretive writing, "This is the spot where…" is descriptive information, not interpretation. Management-stewardship messages are a form of informational writing and can exhibit more than one element of interpretive writing. See the examples in Chapter 7.

Creative writing is an artistic expression that evokes sensory impressions and images. Novels and poetry are in this category. *As with creative writing, interpretive writing draws on metaphor, analogies, comparisons, imagery, visualizations, and making emotional connections.*

Interpretive writing is a blending of these styles in various proportions, depending on the topic. Regardless of how the styles are blended, the resulting message must be goal-directed and pro-social in order for it to be interpretive.

INTERPRETIVE WRITING DEFINED

Themes

All good writing is thematic, regardless of the genre. Theme development is fundamental to all writing styles. Themes make writing clear. I have learned in my "Art of Interpretive Writing" workshops that many writers are unfamiliar with the structure of a theme. Most consider a topic a theme. The topic is the subject matter of the written piece and is written as a sentence fragment. Topics are vague, offering no direction about the pending storyline. Consider this list of topics:

Lake Mead National Recreation Area
People of the Mohave
Palm Trees of the Tropics
Mammals of North America
Desert Snakes
Florida Alligators

Notice that each only tells the subject matter. Every topic can have many storylines depending on what you want to communicate to your readers.

A theme, in contrast, is the principle message about the topic that you want to communicate to your readers. According to Dr. Sam Ham, author of *Environmental Interpretation*, a theme implicitly asks the question, "So, what?" If you consider the topic "Florida Alligators," ask the question, "So what about Florida alligators?"

Dr. William J. Lewis, in his book *Interpreting for Park Visitors*, suggests that a theme should be stated as a short, simple, complete sentence; contain only one idea; reveal the overall direction of the writing; and be interestingly worded. Applying Ham's "So what?" to Lewis' operational definition, I can write several themes for the topic "Florida Alligators."

Florida alligators are coming to get us.
Florida alligators are highly evolved predators.
Florida alligators are a management success story.
Florida alligators deserve our protection.
Florida alligators make terrible pets.

Note that each of these themes can be followed by the word "because" in order to develop sub-themes. For example:

Florida alligators are coming to get us because they are overpopulated.
Florida alligators are coming to get us because they do not like us.
Florida alligators are coming to get us because they are attracted to our pets.
Florida alligators are coming to get us because they are maniacal killers.

Each of the sentences is a sub-theme, and taken in total, I have the structure of a text. The theme not only tells me how the text is structured, it lets me know that if I write about alligator purses, I have wandered away from my theme—and the goal of the message.

The Genre of Interpretive Writing

Interpretive writing is a definable genre. It has characteristics similar to other styles of writing, but there are differences. I have selected five elements that I believe to be essential to true interpretive writing. I chose these because I believe they follow the writing traditions of some of our most notable interpretive writers, because they are measurable, and they are essentials known to most front-line interpreters, planners, and managers.

Interpretive writing is a style because its elements are recognizable, because of its use of grammar, and because it performs the basic functions of interpretation. I define interpretive grammar later in Chapter 5, "Conventions and Rules for Interpretive Writers" and Chapter 19, "The Editing Process." Here, I will address the basic functions of interpretive writing. I like these elements because they are measurable. I can identify whether these functions exist in a text and make an assessment to what degree they are present. Because they are quantifiable, they are guideposts for improving a written piece. Later, I will introduce measurement instruments that use these elements and apply the instruments to several writing samples.

1. **Interpretive writing is goal-directed.** It fulfills a purpose. The language moves the reader towards higher-level understanding, stewardship, and/or life-long learning. It challenges the reader to be able to do, think, or feel something that they did not do, think, or feel before reading the message.

2. **Interpretive writing relates to something tangible.** The tangible is an

artifact, a resource, an object, a relic, or a factual description of an event. A noun or a noun phrase identifies the tangible. In my workshops, I offer a man's pocket watch for examination and ask participants to generate a list of tangible attributes. Their responses include: *it is round, it is silver, it has black numbers printed on a white face, it has the words "Ball Company" on the white face, it weighs three ounces, it makes a ticking sound.* All of the responses are measurable or verifiable.

3. **The attributes of the tangible are associated with its intangible qualities, the inherent meanings of the tangible.** Audiences have identifiable characteristics that overlap with other audiences or are mutually exclusive. Each audience perceives reality through a set of mental filters that accepts and rejects various external stimulations. Demographic characteristics define audiences. The characteristics include how audiences respond to external forces, and their internal belief structure.

    I ask participants in my workshop to share the intangible attributes of the man's pocket watch. Their responses include: *it reminds me of my grandfather, it makes me feel anxiety because time is ticking away, I think of heirlooms in my family, it looks old so it must be valuable.* Whereas everyone can agree on the verifiable and measurable tangible attributes, there are insurmountable differences between the ways the participants perceive the intangible attributes.

4. **The meaningful qualities of the tangible are associated with a universal concept.** These are big ideas about which almost everyone on Earth has some understanding. Examples of universal concepts include fear, love, peace, change, life, wonder, family, history, trade, and death. The universals listed by participants for the pocket watch are *family, love, work, and time.*

5. **Interpretive writing creates an opportunity for the reader to form an intellectual and emotional connection with the tangible.** The connection is essential in order for the reader to care about the tangible. In my workshops, I tell a story about the watch that relates its history. I then connect the facts with an emotional component built on the universal concept of family.

What does interpretive writing achieve? The intent of interpretive writing is to tell a story with as much richness as told through oral tradition. Effective interpretive writing makes a connection between the artifact and the reader. It compels the reader to think about and view his or her world from a different perspective.

Interpretive writing makes the resource relevant to the life of the reader by presenting tangible attributes as opportunities to discovering meanings. It enlightens, enriches, challenges, and inspires the reader by focusing on intangibles, targeting universal concepts, and influencing the reader to make emotional connections with the resource.

Writing projects are interpretive when they have the five elements of interpretation and they are thematic. This structure gives writers a framework for outlining interpretive messages, and it gives reviewers criteria by which they can assess the product.

Questions you may have are, "Must every written piece have all five elements in order to be interpretive?" and, "How is it possible for a museum label of 12 words to have all five elements?" Think of the entire exhibit in the museum as the interpretive story. Each label tells part of the story. The role of one label might be to make an intellectual/emotional connection. The purpose of another label may be to discuss the tangible attributes of an artifact. The labels in their entirety must have all five elements in order for the exhibit to be interpretive. The planner, writer, and design team members decide the order in which to tell the story.

The following photographs of panels in Waterton Lakes National Park, Alberta, Canada, illustrate this point. The first photograph shows the placement of five panels. The panels are sequential in telling a thematic story about the pieces of a puzzle that come together to form the dynamics of a forest environment. The second photograph shows a detail of the first panel in the sequence. The role of each panel is to tell part of the story. Consequently, the five elements of interpretive writing are not found in each panel, but found in the collection of the five panels.

It is not surprising that interpretive writing elements exist in almost every style of writing. Interpretive writing shares attributes with other writing styles. Science writing, for instance, is defined when it answers the question, "Why is this important to me?" Creative writing deals with a universal, such as, love, conflict, wealth, or power. Promotional writing is intended to elicit a response.

In Autumn 2004, my son attended a freshman English composition class at the University of Montana. As with many "101" classes, it was taught by a graduate teaching assistant. Dustin was pleased when he showed me the grade he received on his first composition, but added, "The teaching assistant scolded the class, saying she was disappointed that most of the compositions were descriptive, and that she could not distinguish universals or a purpose for the majority of the papers." I was pleased to hear her criteria.

Writing with a purpose, focusing on universal concepts while making emotional connections, is not new. Consider Rachel Carson's piece from *The Sense of Wonder*.

In my mail recently was a letter that bore eloquent testimony to the lifelong durability of a sense of wonder. It came from a reader who asked advice on choosing a seacoast spot for a vacation, a place wild enough that she might spend her days roaming beaches unspoiled by civilization, exploring the world that is old but ever new.

Regretfully she excluded the rugged northern shores. She loved the shore all her life, she said, but climbing over the rocks of Maine might be difficult, for an eighty-ninth birthday would soon arrive. As I put down her letter I was warmed by the fires of wonder and amazement that still burned brightly in her youthful mind and spirit, just as they must have fourscore years ago.

Carson wrote an emotional story based upon the universal concept of learning. She wrote the story for parents with the purpose of encouraging life-long learning for their children.

Another example that shows elements of interpretive writing appear in good writing is found in this excerpt from wildlife biologist Aldo Leopold's *A Sand County Almanac*.

Every July I watch eagerly a certain graveyard that I pass in driving to and from my farm. It is time for a prairie birthday, and in one corner of this graveyard lives a surviving celebrant of that once-important event.

It is an ordinary graveyard...extraordinary only in being triangular instead of square, and in harboring, within the sharp angle of its fence, a pine-point remnant of the native prairie on which the graveyard was established in the 1840s. Heretofore unreachable by scythe or mower, this yard-spare relic of original Wisconsin gives birth, each July, to a man-high stalk of compass plant or cutleaf Silphium, spangled with saucer-sized yellow blooms resembling sunflowers. It is the sole remnant of this plant along the highway, and perhaps the sole remnant in the western half of our country. What a thousand acres of Silphiums looked like when they tickled the bellies of the buffalo is a question never again to be answered, and perhaps not even asked.

This year I found the Silphium in first bloom on 24 July, a week later than usual....

When I passed the graveyard again on 3 August, the fence had been removed by a road crew, and the Silphium cut. It is easy now to predict the future; for a few years my Silphium will try in vain to rise above the mowing machine, and then it will die. With it will die the prairie epoch....

This is one little episode in the funeral of the native flora, which in turn is an episode in the funeral of the floras of the world.

Leopold's story involves a resource (the compass plant), a universal (death), and intellectual and emotional connections (related to the loss of not only one plant but the floras of the world).

My son's experience with his writing teacher, as well as the anecdotes from Leopold and Carson, illustrate that good writers apply elements of interpretive writing. Once familiar with the five elements, you will see them in other media, including television news reports, National Public Radio stories, magazine articles, and Web sites.

Many media feature other attributes of good story-telling, including humor, relevance, metaphors, quotations, good action verbs, and proper grammar. Of these other attributes, proper grammar is the only one that has easily definable assessment criteria.

Interpretive writing then, as a genre, has a specific structure. Assessing the existence of five elements in interpretive projects gives interpretive writers and team members a tool to determine the potential effectiveness of their message.

KNOW YOUR AUDIENCE

Communication Models

Little was considered about how people interact until the late 1940s. At that time, Bell Telephone Company research scientists were challenged to investigate how to get maximum telephone line capacity with minimum distortion (noise) caused by extraneous electromagnetic radiation.

The researchers had no interest in the semantic meaning of a message or its effect on the listener. They were not concerned whether the telephone line carried business conversations or intimate talk. They aimed at solving the technical problems of the transfer of sound. A schematic model of their work shows a one-way flow of information. Their concern was to keep noise out of the message.

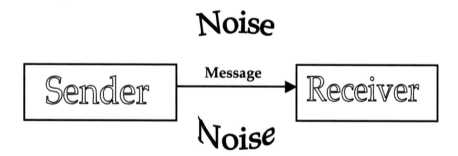

Working independently, Massachusetts Institute of Technology (MIT) scientists realized that noise was actually a form of feedback. The noise, to them, was parallel to what happens in communication machines. Receiving feedback was a challenge during World War II. During the war, anti-aircraft firing systems that would adjust future trajectory of bullets by reinstating results of past performance were developed. Researchers had learned that feedback is a way to introduce learning into the system.

Social scientists in the early 1950s became aware of the work conducted by

Bell Laboratories and MIT and blended their ideas into a model to explain everyday, face-to-face communications. From Bell's work, social scientists created the preceding model, where there is a sender and receiver, without a feedback loop. Social scientists took the MIT ideas and developed a model with a feedback loop associated with every verbal interaction.

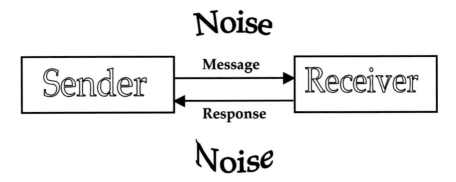

Using the MIT idea as a springboard, social scientists have continued to refine the message-response model to include non-verbal feedback and adapted delivery elements. Alison Grinder and Sue McCoy discuss feedback and adapted delivery as it applies to interpreters in their book, *The Good Guide*. They state, "Feedback moves from visitors to guides and from guides to visitors. It can tell us, by a number of cues, how well we are doing in inspiring visitors and in communicating information to them."

Decoding feedback allows front-line interpreters to modify their presentations to better meet the needs of audiences.

Front-Line Interpretation

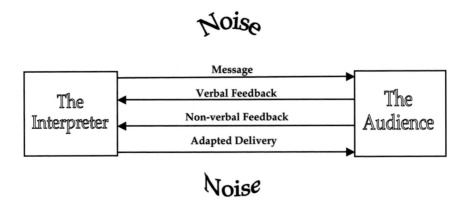

The all-encompassing element in this model is the ever-present element of noise. Noise assumes many manifestations. As a front-line interpreter, I must constantly adjust my presentation to external influences such as children in the front row of a campfire arena swinging their legs and kicking rocks, or an RV passing while I am in period clothing, or visitors arriving late to a program and disrupting members in the group. Noise can also include non-verbal communication. Smiles, crossed arms, eye contact, and posture are among the myriad elements that can be distracting during a presentation.

Non-verbal communication, as well as verbal communication messages from audiences, allows front-line interpreters to adjust presentation delivery and messages while a presentation is taking place. Unlike front-line interpreters, interpretive writers have no such feedback mechanism.

Written Interpretation

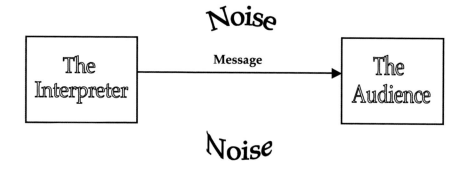

Noise is the critical element in this model. It is a negative part of the communication process, yet I use it to strengthen my writing. I ask reviewers when noise is apparent as they are reading my copy. At what point did outside influences distract them? At what part of the text did their mind wander? Their answers tell me where I need to rewrite the copy to make it more engaging to my reader.

Close understanding of audience attributes is necessary in interpretation. It is critical in written interpretation. Front-line interpreters can assess verbal interaction and non-verbal audience feedback in real time and change their presentation for better effect. Interpretive writers get delayed audience feedback, if any. When writers do receive audience feedback, it is rare that they can adjust the message. I have found that understanding how the audience views a resource is critical to being able to write effective text. This allows me to anticipate feedback as if I were operating within the front-line interpretation model, the more effective of the two.

Who is Your Audience?

A detailed understanding of the needs, wants, and problems of your audience allows you to author effective interpretive messages. Understanding what your readers want and their socio-economic characteristics allows you to address the intangible attributes of your resource to meet their interests. Consider the following before developing your message: What do your readers want from you? What are the characteristics of your audience?

What do your readers want from you? Audiences are defined, in part, by what they seek. Observing visitors at the Buffalo Bill Historical Center in Cody, Wyoming, is instructive regarding audience preferences. The center houses four museums and an art gallery: the Whitney Gallery of Western Art, the Buffalo Bill Museum, the Plains Indian Museum, the Cody Firearms Museum, and the Draper Museum of Natural History.

As visitors enter, they go to one of the museums or the art gallery. There are identifiable characteristics of visitors who only attend the Plains Indian Museum. They are looking for interpretation that addresses only that topic. Learning who these people are allows the interpretive writer to write messages that target their specific interests. The grammar and media approach may be different for visitors at the Draper Museum of Natural History than the Cody Firearms Museum.

Economic status, education, race, shopping preferences, recreational preferences, age, and family composition are among the countless ways to group and define audiences. The following are three ways to group and examine audiences.

1. School Groups
- Elementary school children (grades K–6)
- High school children (grades 7–12)
- University students (high school graduates attending college programs)
- Home school (children of any school age who do not attend a formal public or private school)

2. Family Groups
- Single persons (no children)
- Single family (one parent with children)
- Grandparent-parents (grandparents as providers of grandchildren)
- Two-parent families with children
- Traditional extended family (mother, father, children, grandparents, relatives)
- Single parent with children (one or more children)
- Adult groups without children (young couples)
- Empty nesters (adults in late 40s who have grown children no longer living with them)
- Elderly or retired visitors (visitors over 70 traveling as couples or in organized tours)

3. Generational Groups

People born at approximately the same time share similar worldviews. Each generation has defining events, such as war, prosperity, or disease. Consumer data firms like Acxiom and trade magazines such as *American Demographics* provide in-depth regional and local information about communities and populations. Listed below is the U.S. population divided into five generations. Each generation has a brief generalized description of its characteristics and a suggestion of how they respond to media messages.

1.   The War Generation, ages 80 and higher, identifies with multi-generational entertainment, soft adventure, photo safaris, and young and old product messages.

2.   The Silent Generation, ages 65 to 79, identifies with right verses wrong, "I've earned my rewards, and it's time for a little pleasure" messages. They are well educated and affluent. They are members of church groups, veterans groups, and country clubs.

3.   Baby Boomers, ages 48 to 64, identify with messages that relate to instant gratification, messages that are quick to read, and messages that provide choices. They like non-consumptive sports like golf and tennis. Many are members of art associations and they like to attend sporting events.

4.   Generation X, ages 27 to 47, identifies with messages that are straight-forward, non-manipulative, romantic, and ethnic. They like to go to museums, shop for quality merchandise, and travel.

5.   The Millennium Generation, ages 26 and under, identifies with empowering messages, messages that show optimism and point to stewardship. They like messages that help them see how to change the world. They enjoy outdoor activities and sports events.

Based on the characteristics outlined in the generational groups, I have asked participants in my "Art of Interpretive Writing" workshops to write museum labels for Crayola crayons. The challenge: write a museum label of 30 words or fewer targeting a specific group of readers. The goal of the message is to interpret that there has been little or no change in crayons since they were invented in 1903. Below are some of their contributions.

The War Generation

Crayola Crayon, circa 1903
Burnt Sienna? Brick Red? Forest Green? What was your favorite color? You spent
hours creating with these colorful pieces of wax. More than four generations have
expressed their artistry with Crayola Crayons. The best traditions need no change.
                    —Beverly Slavens, Ouachita Baptist University, Arkadelphia, Arkansas

A Rare Classic
Mmmm, the smell of a fresh box of crayons.... They are the same today as
they were 80 years ago. Escaping with only a few changes, they continue to
delight. Just visit a kindergarten class at craft time to be taken back to your
own age of innocence.
                    —Kelly Mulvihill, Janet Huckabee Arkansas River Valley Nature Center

Baby Boomers

Crayola Crayons: A Twentieth-Century Success Story
Remember when your parents gave you crayons as a child? Children today are
playing with virtually the same crayon as children in 1903. While many things have
changed since the days you were frustrated at having to "stay within the lines,"
some technologies have remained the same.
                    —Billy Strasser, Klondike Gold Rush National Historical Park

Crayons: Innovation Since 1903
Crayons have changed little despite technology advances. Why? Because crayons
work—even the broken pieces! Remember coloring with kids down the block?
Even now with your grandchildren you can both marvel at the genius of Crayola.
                    —Betsy A. Leonard, Parachute, Colorado

The Silent Generation

The Blue Crayon
He thanked his grandson. The blue sky and green grass coloring brought
tears as he remembered another drawing years ago that carried him home.
                    —Cyndi Eide, BLM, Billings, Montana

Generation X

CDs, DVDs, MP3s and PSPs
Almost daily modern devices have grown to become what they are today. One has
not changed: Crayola crayons have refused to grow up.
                    —Heather Currey, Oregon State Parks, Port Orford

Crayons
Shopping for school supplies, it was a challenge, could you get Mom to buy the BIG box with the sharpener on the back? Since 1903, crayons have released our creativity.

—Virginia D. Bourdeau, Associate Professor,
Oregon State University 4-H Specialist

These examples show minor changes to the message depending on the characteristics of the audiences. It is not possible to know everyone—each belief, group of interests, education—but it is possible to study the demographics in which they fit. Many interest groupings are self-selected, such as outdoor enthusiasts, weavers, and amateur historians. Self-selected groupings offer the most precision for identifying distinctiveness.

The best way to find out audience characteristics is to ask visitors who they are, where they came from, and what their interests are. You can do this through a research firm or informally. Research firms are expensive, but give good reliable data. Asking the questions yourself provides greater intimacy with your audience and a better understanding of how they view the subject you are writing about.

The most effective pathway to writing good interpretive messages is to understand your audiences' intangible perspectives of the resource. Recognizing the uniqueness of your audience will guide you to concentrate on what is important to the demographic.

CONVENTIONS AND
RULES FOR
INTERPRETIVE WRITERS

Douglas Adams' *Hitchhiker's Guide to the Galaxy* has one rule: DON'T PANIC. Reducing all of the rules for interpretive writers to one rule would state, "Keep it short," with a codicil; some rules can be broken, but not this one. I like to share this example in my writing workshops. It illustrates that you can include all the important elements of writing and meet a goal without being wordy.

> In a literature class the students were challenged to be concise and write a story that included the ingredients nobility, emotion, sex, religion, and mystery. A student wrote: "'My god!' Cried the duchess, 'I'm pregnant. Who did it?'"

Singer/songwriter, Willie Nelson, points out in his book *The Tao of Willie* that "the shorter you can make a song and still get your point across, the better the chances of airplay." He goes on to say, "My bunch of songwriter buddies—like Roger Miller and Kris Kristofferson—were taught to say what you wanted to say in six or nine lines.... That helped us concentrate on the lines we wanted to use and forces us to put more thought into them. I'd sooner have three great verses than 30 mediocre ones; if nothing else, it makes the song easier to remember." Easier to remember is what interpretive writers want, too. Establish a formula that limits word count. Force yourself to be succinct. If your audience is willing to dedicate time to read a 30-word museum label, but you have provided a 75-word label, then you have written 45 words only for yourself.

Keeping messages short does not mean simplifying them to the point of not being useful. It does mean finding the correct words and syntax to have the best impact. Mark Twain's letter to D. W. Bowser of March 20,1880 highlights this point: "...plain, simple language, short words, and brief sentences. That is the way to write English—it is the modern way and the best way. Stick to it; don't let fluff and flowers and verbosity creep in."

Some of the content of this book comes from my experiences conducting "Art of Interpretive Writing" workshops. As discussed in the preface, I selected the title of the workshop to emphasize that interpretive writing is an art form.

Oil painters select colors from their pallet and blend them into a visual expression, with appropriate proportions and mixtures bringing life to the painting. Reliance on any one color distracts from the intended message. In much the same way, interpretive writers compose messages that work. The only criterion that matters for an interpretive writer is whether the message promotes a positive action with the intended audience. As such, it is appropriate for interpretive writers to use whatever tools they have to meet their goals. The following rules, common to most grammar books, are in two categories: rules that should never be broken and rules that can be broken to meet interpretive goals. Remember, you have the right to break the rules only after you know how to apply the rules in conventional settings.

Rules that Must Not Be Broken

1. Consider all interpretive writing as formal writing. Your thought patterns and everyday speech are informal. You should not write in the same patterns in which you speak. Use extra care in selecting words and syntax so as to increase your chances of communicating your messages.

2. Capitalize only proper nouns. Glacier National Park, Bonneville Dam, and Robert E. Lee are examples. Words like butterfly are not proper nouns, unless used in a name like Butterfly McQueen.

3. Verbs must agree with their subjects.

4. Keep the writing short.

5. Be specific. Ask yourself, "What is the one thing you want your readers to remember in five minutes, five hours, five days, five years?" Write to that one point.

6. Never use run-on sentences. Most grammar and spell-checking programs will highlight run-on sentences. Break the run-on sentence into two or more, or re-write the sentence.

7. Use spell-check software. Most readers can tell if you misspell *mispell*, or write *cemetary* for *cemetery*. You might get by with misspelling words in informal email messages, but formal writing does not allow spelling errors.

8. Learn when to use affect and effect; less and fewer; lay, lie, laid, and laying. Numerous English grammar books tell proper usage. Mainstream popular books listed in the selected resources include *100 Words Almost Everyone*

Confuses & Misuses, When Good People Write Bad Sentences, Sin and Syntax, The Elements of Style, and *On Writing Well.*

9. Use either one or three exclamation points, never two, four, or more. One exclamation point is enough for emphasis. Three is the convention for a heavy weighting in informal writing. Two exclamation points make no sense, and more than three is superfluous.

10. Quotation marks go on the outside of punctuation, except with colons and semicolons.

11. Proofread your first draft before you share it with a colleague. Keyboards and word processors are not aware of your intended message. It is easy to keyboard the word *from* when you meant the word *form.* Spell checkers do not alert you to consider whether you want the word *ask* rather than *as.* The only way to catch these errors is to develop a proofreading pattern. Scanning the lines backwards or reading the words aloud as they appear on the screen are two proofreading techniques.

12. Restrict the number of questions. Readers like questions, provided they understand the questions are leading somewhere. Questions need purpose. Limit open-ended questions; readers like the closure that answers provide. For a discussion on question categories, refer to *Personal Interpretation: Connecting Your Audience to Heritage Resources* by Lisa Brochu and Tim Merriman.

Rules that Can Be Broken to Meet Interpretive Goals

1. All sentences begin with a capital letter and end with a punctuation mark, such as a period, an explanation mark, or a question mark.

2. Keep sentence fragments to a minimum. Sentence fragments are good when they limit text word count or encourage readers to complete the sentences in their own way. However, fragments distract from interpretive messages in long texts.

3. Use descriptive and emotive words in lieu of adjectives. Saying that it was a beautiful sunset gives little information for the reader to envision your image. Instead, describe the sunset, make comparisons, and use emotive language.

4. Resist using adverbs. Words ending in "ly" contribute nothing to make a text powerful. They are soft words without clarity. If "he quickly ran," then just how fast did he run? Adverbs do not answer to what degree or extent.

Precision is vital in interpretive writing. Eliminate the need for adverbs with action verbs. Instead of: "The bobcat went quickly…" try, "The bobcat hurried…" or "The bobcat bolted…." Bolted and hurried are action verbs. Action verbs create a picture for the reader.

5. Avoid using prepositions to end sentences. This is common in everyday language, but will stand out as a distraction in formal writing.

6. Keep the same point of view throughout the interpretive piece. Shifting from first-person to second-person to third-person is common in everyday speech and news editorials, but it is not appropriate in formal writing. Select one point of view and keep it throughout the text.

7. Do not start a sentence with a conjunction. This is common practice in informal writing. Consider interpretive writing as formal writing, and sentences must not begin with a conjunction.

8. Limit alliteration. Alliteration can be fun to read, but the rhythm can be distracting.

9. Limit parenthetical remarks. They may increase clarity, but as punctuation are speed bumps to easy reading.

10. Contractions are unnecessary. They are informal language and should not appear in interpretive writing.

11. Your audience must understand all foreign words and phrases you use. English does not have all the words and phrases to successfully communicate all emotions and concepts. Therefore, a combination with other languages can be effectual in relating your message. Know your audience and use language that your readers understand.

12. Avoid ampersands. An ampersand is a typographic symbol for the word, *and* (&). Although common in advertising notices, signs, and business names, I have never met anyone who could freehand an ampersand with ease. Interpretive writers should avoid using ampersands because they are associated with informal notices. The brain decodes the ampersand as the word *and*, so, go ahead and just use the word.

13. Shun abbreviations. There are various accepted ways to abbreviate words and phrases. For instance, California is often abbreviated, Calif., Cal., or CA, (although CA was promoted by the United States Postal Service as a symbol, it is frequently used as an abbreviation). Like the ampersand symbol, the

mind must decode the abbreviation for it to make sense in its context, slowing reading. Unfamiliar and archaic abbreviations are distracting.

14. Use the apostrophe in its proper place and omit it when it's not needed. If an apostrophe is needed, you will be able to invert the word order and say "of" or "of the": black bear's appetite; the appetite of the black bear. I recommend Lynne Truss' *Eats, Shoots, & Leaves* for a light-touch dissertation on the angst of an apostrophe stickler. Apostrophes are often used in the wrong place because the writer is not aware of grammar. Some writers leave apostrophes out of their messages for brevity. Most readers have a basic understanding of apostrophes and can be mislead when they are missing or out of order.

15. Select short quotations that enhance your storyline. Be aware of the popularity of the person quoted and if the quote appears frequently in other media. Overused quotations become cliché. Quotations from Rachel Carson, Aldo Leopold, John Muir, Mark Twain, and Walt Whitman that connect to broad audiences are overused, and frequently quoted at great length. Passages that are authoritative from recognizable persons are sometimes the best way to communicate your message. Select the quotations with deep consideration.

16. Avoid colloquialisms. They are words or phases that come from everyday speech and do not belong in formal writing.

17. Using vernacular restricts your audience. Vernacular is everyday language of the people in a particular region of the country as opposed to colloquial language accepted by people in all regions. In my area of Montana, people refer to elk antlers as elk horns. They know the difference but prefer saying elk horns in their everyday language. An interpretive sign that uses the term *elk horns* could confuse readers from outside the region.

18. Avoid cliches. They are non-specific, trite expressions that confuse readers. Review the list of cliches beginning on page 30 to better identify those that appear in your writing.

I have found that writers who follow these rules create the most succinct, readable, and engaging messages. Interpretive writing is a recognizable genre that is defined, in part, by its use of grammar. Some conventions can be broken, some cannot. Interpretation is a process of communicating a message with a purpose. Interpretive writing is a formal process of communicating with a consistent use of rules based on good grammar and interpretive techniques. The previous rules I believe are the most important for helping to define the interpretive writing genre.

A Collection of Cliches

The following is a sample of clichés I have found in various interpretive texts. Review your writing to see if you are using trite expressions. If so, consider being more explicit.

A. about the same / above board / absolutely fantastic / according to plan / according to the experts / across the board / after the break / against the grain / against the odds / ages ago / ahead of his time / alive and well / all for a good cause / all for one / all men are created equal / all or nothing / all right then / all smoke and mirrors/all the time / all time great / all to the good / all work no play / all clear / all's fair in love and war / almost certain / amazing thing is / an act of faith / and that's that

B. backed into a corner / backs to the wall / bad behavior / bad hair day / bad news / bad reputation / balanced view / balancing act / ball is in your court / ball park figure / barking up the wrong tree / barrel of laughs / basic principles / battle lines / be prepared / beating around the bush / beauty is only skin deep / behave yourself / behind the scenes / below the belt / benefit of the doubt / beside the point / best efforts / best foot forward

C. call it a day / call the shots / call you later / calm before the storm / can't put a finger on it / can't see the forest for the trees / cannot confirm or deny / carbon copy / cards on the table / carry on / cast the first stone / categorically denied / caught me off balance / cause and effect / crunch time / cry for help / crying out / crystal clear / cut and dried

D. damage control / day by day / dead as a door nail / dead end / deemed to be appropriate / deeply concerned / delaying tactics / delicate matter / dictated the terms / divide and conquer / divine inspiration / do away with

E. easy answer / easy as pie / easy come easy go / easy going / easy touch / eating crow / eggs in one basket / element of doubt / environmentally friendly / equal footing / equal opportunities/exact replica / eye witness

F. face the facts / face the music / face up to reality / fact is / fair deal / fall into place / far reaching / far reaching implications / fast and loose / fast expanding / feather your own nest / feel free / final decision / fly by night / fly in the ointment/for future reference/for the moment / for the record

G. game plan / gathering momentum / gave the impression / get a handle on it / get a hold of yourself / get a life / get away with it / get back to you later / ghost town/give a good impression / give it up / give me a break / given the circumstances / given the facts / given the run around/go ahead

H. hand over fist / handful / happy campers / hard fought / hard lesson/hard to believe/have a nice day / have a word / head in the clouds / heads up / healthy cynicism / hear what I say / heart of the matter / hidden agenda

I. I don't follow you / I like it / if you ask me / if you want my honest opinion / if you wouldn't mind / immediate concerns / in addition / in case of emergency / in due course / in essence / in my opinion / in no time / in on the ground floor / in principle / in private / in the balance / in the beginning / in the clear / in the course of time / in the dark / in the nick of time/

J. joint agreement / jump at the chance / jump on the bandwagon / junk food / just a minute / just desserts / just the man I wanted to see / just trying to be friendly

K. keep fit / keep the door open / key player / keynote address / killing time / kiss of death / knock on wood /know what you're talking about

L. lack of clarity / laid to rest / last chance / last drop / last laugh / last stand / last straw/late arrival / laugh a minute / laughing all the way to the bank / law and order / lead balloon / leading me on / leading question / leave it to you / leave out in the cold

M. made in heaven / made a mess of it / made a point / maintain the status quo / major upset / make my day / make a killing/make a mountain out of a molehill / make ends meet / make it clear / make it work / mark my words / mass movement / mass production / matter of fact

N. natural order / near miss / near thing / neck and neck / need to know / need the need to know basis / needless to say / never too late / never again / never been found / new age / new beginnings / new image / new information / new to you / new world order / next of kin / next stop / nice one / nice try / nick of time / nine lives / nine out of ten / nip it in the bud / no offense intended / no worries / no sense of humor / no free lunches / no change / no alternative / no argument

O. of course / off hand / off the wall / on board / on top of the world / on the same page / on average/on my own terms / on the back burner / on the basis/on the contrary / on the defensive / on the ground / on the lookout / on the money / on the other hand / on the spot/on the tip of my tongue / on top of it / on your way / once in a lifetime / once in a blue moon / one thing after the next / one of the key things is / one of these days/one step at a time / open minded / opening moves/out of control / out of focus / out of order

P. package deal / painted himself into a corner / Pandora's box / panic button/paper exercise / pardon my French / pencil in/pick of the crop / pick up where we left off /

pie in the sky / plain as day / plain as the nose on your face / playing with fire / point of view / power play / practice makes perfect/precious time/pressing the right buttons / pressing ahead / pretty sure

Q. quality of life / quality service / question mark / question of time / quick recap / quick turnaround / quick witted / quick and the dead / quick as a flash / quiet word / quite natural / quite common

R. rabble rouser / race war / raining cats and dogs / raise the roof/rank and file / re-inventing the wheel / read between the lines / reading between the lines/really pleased/red tape / red neck / red carpet treatment / reduction in numbers / refused to cooperate / relatively straightforward / remain optimistic / repeat performance

S. say what you like / scaling down / scorched earth / scraping the bottom of the barrel / second guess / security risk/see reason / see through it / self evident / self preservation / sell out / serious proposition / serious disagreement / sexually explicit / shooting fish in a barrel / shot in the dark / side issues/side by side / sign of the times / sign on the dotted line / simple example / simple pleasures / simple fact / simple truth

T. take it easy / take your time / take the lead / take advantage of / take that / take a stand / take a break / take a rain check / take it or leave it / take my word / take a chance / taken for granted / taking this too seriously / taking steps / tall tales / target audience / team work / thanks for nothing/the bottom line / the end of the road / the thing is / the off chance / the one and only / the perfect solution / the problem is / the right thing / the question is / the third degree / the writing on the wall / the silent majority

U. ultimate objective / under the skin / under the weather /under the impression / under the thumb / under pressure / under the rules / underlying principles / unfair advantage / unforeseeable circumstances / up tight / up to date/urgent need / use your head / useful lessons

W. wait and see / wait a minute / wasn't my fault / watch your step/water under the bridge/watered down / way of life/way out / we can work it out / well done/went the full circle / what can only be described as / what goes around comes around / what can I get you / what's the problem / what's new / what's what / what's that got to do with it / what's on your mind / who cares / who's next / whole truth

Y-Z. you know what they say / you can be sure of it / you can hardly blame him / you can't be too careful / you know what I mean/zero tolerance

PART TWO

how to

THE WRITING PROCESS

There are myriad approaches to writing, and countless authors, teachers, and colleagues giving their opinion how to approach and complete a writing project. Listen to them and glean wisdom that you can incorporate into your own process. Writer Jessamyn West pointed out, "There is no royal path to good writing; and such paths as they exist do not lead through neat critical gardens, various as they are, but through the jungles of self, the world, and of craft."

There is not one definitive way to write. However, everyone agrees on some aspects of the process. The following list of ideas is deceptive; it suggests that the process is longitudinal. It is not. It also suggests that each aspect is equal in importance—they are not. The writing process is dynamic and free-flowing rather than a formula. I suggest the following:

- Create a list of ideas that you are interested in writing about.

- Select a set of these ideas and organize them into logical progression.

- Research the ideas. Collect salient information.

- Write a first draft.

- Self-edit the first draft.

- Rewrite. Great interpretive messages are not written, they are rewritten.

- Peer review. Give it to a friend, colleague, or stranger to read. Make sure they understand the audience and the purpose of the text.

- Rewrite.

- Edit and proof. Either self-edit and proof your copy or give it to someone else.

- Revise into a final product.

Most of the writers I know declare they spend the majority of their time researching. For them, the writing process begins with research rather than creating a list of ideas. They also state that they return to research frequently after review.

The list also suggests limited rewrite and revision. In fact, rewrite and revision commonly occur countless times.

Finally, if you want to be a good writer, read. Be familiar with several authors and their styles. Learning to be a good writer often means mimicking good authors. Learn how others use verbs, adjectives, nouns, and prepositions. Study how authors mold dynamic sentences.

The Interpretive Writing Process

The interpretive writing process has four parts: planning, interpretive writing elements, layout, and editing. This book is a treatment of the writing and the editing parts. The facets are inclusive and consideration of the planning process and layout fundamentals are important to understanding the interpretive writing process.

Interpretation is purposeful, whether front-line or written. Lisa Brochu, author of *Interpretive Planning,* and John Veverka, author of *Interpretive Master Planning,* have addressed the resolute nature of interpretation from their own perspectives. They agree that effective interpretive products are a result of connecting the message to a fundamental purpose. The purpose finds its origins in either the organic act of the site, the master plan of the site, or the singular goal of the communication. Larry Beck and Ted Cable point out in *Interpretation for the 21st Century* that the "overall interpretive program must be capable of attracting support—financial, volunteer, political, administrative—whatever support is needed for the program to flourish." Applied to interpretive writing, the content of the message must target a purpose intended to bring about a positive reaction or emotive change in the reader. This does not preclude that some interpretive writing can be just for fun, if that is the purpose of the text.

The interpretive writing process begins with planning and a set of associated questions. All interpretive writers should ask the following questions:

How does the intended message relate to a goal? To write without a goal is to write for recreation.

What is the desired theme of the message? Good writing is thematic. Almost every sample of good writing, whether a novel, Web site, or a brochure, has a specific message that is intended to be remembered. The advertising world calls this the take-away point. The specific message can be expressed as a thematic statement. I like the way William J. Lewis expresses the value of a theme in his book *Interpreting for Park Visitors*: "At the completion of any interpretive presentation, the audience should be able to tell you what was said by summarizing it in one sentence. This sentence is the theme, the central or key idea of any presentation." I can apply his assertion to writing, and state: "In one sentence, the reader should be able to tell you to your satisfaction the central point of the message."

Is a text more effective than personal interpretation in communicating the message? In the course of social development, the written word replaced personal interaction. Before there were ubiquitous written texts, troubadours, tellers of epic poems like the *Ramayana* and *Beowulf*, and people relating fairy tales and fables were the conveyers of social norms, history, and responsibilities. The presentation of the written word has evolved. Today, ideas expressed through writing appear in radio scripts, Web sites, digital video, and audio recordings. Interpretive planners realize the cost-effectiveness of media over personal interpretation. Planners rely on media to communicate regulations and interpret resources in place of and along with an interpreter. William Lewis states in *Interpreting for Park Visitors* that the reason people participate in park activities is to learn something they otherwise would not and "to be with someone who will communicate with them." People want personal interaction. Do not take it for granted that writing a text is the only means of conveying your message. Consider why you are willing to replace personal interpretation. If non-personal interpretation is the most effective means of relating the message, then move forward and write an interpretive text that talks to the reader.

In what media will the message appear? Go to any visitor center, nature center, museum, arboretum, or park entrance station and ask for their brochure. You might be asked, "Which one?" It seems like every site manager thinks it is incumbent to have one or more brochures to interpret the resource. I am not sure whether most managers question if visitors read the brochures. It appears to be a given that a site must have a brochure that interprets the resource. Interpretive writing goes beyond writing for the static media of brochures, museum labels, and wayside displays. Interpretive writing now includes writing for dynamic media forms like Web sites, digital transmissions, and interactive computer programs. Each has a nuance separating it from the traditional, static forms of interpretive writing. For example, that is why Web pages require short sentences. People can read more than twice as fast from a reflected surface like this page than they can from a projected surface like a computer screen. Be prepared to write for media other than brochures and signage.

How will the text appear in its final form? Planners, editors, and designers are your team members. The effectiveness of the message you are writing depends on the skills and talents of each member. A clear goal provided by a planner allows you to write a strong theme statement. A capable editor and proofreader assures an errorless message that captivates your reader. A gifted designer selects the correct fonts, point sizes, color schemes, graphics, and visual balance to augment your text and attract readers. Knowing how the text will appear helps you select headlines, verbs, and descriptive language that enhances the design.

Who is the audience? There is no such thing as a general audience. If you believe that people from every demographic read your text, think about the people who do not visit your park, nature center, museum, stop along your byway, or see your newspaper column. People with identifiable characteristics slow their recreational vehicles from 65 miles per hour to a stop in one-half mile to read a historic marker. Those people have demographic attributes that may be different from people who visit the annual winter solstice celebration at your nature center. Know your audience. Study their characteristics and find out what they are looking for. Business corporations are leaders in understanding demographics and how to write messages. Interpretive writers need an intimate understanding of their audiences' characteristics in order to build messages that target their audiences' specific interests. Beck and Cable state that "interpretive writing should address what readers would like to know…." An interpretive writer must assess what the audience wants to know and write a text that targets the audience characteristics.

Interpretive Planning by Lisa Brochu and Interpretive Master Planning by John Veverka provide you with an understanding of the role of the planner in the writing process. Sam Ham's Environmental Interpretation presents basic instruction in media design. These authors can give you a deeper understanding of the role of your interpretive writing team.

A Planning Perspective
adapted from Interpretive Planning by Brochu

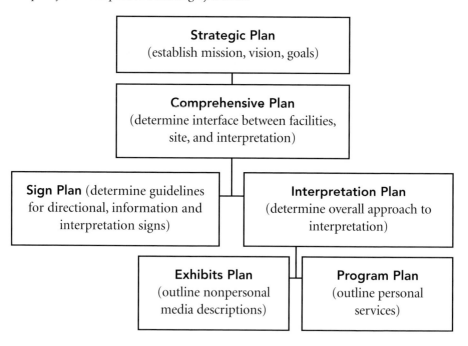

Case Study: *Why planning is important to the interpretive writing process.*

This wayside display is along Montana Highway 308, between Red Lodge and Belfry.

Smith Mine Disaster

Smoke pouring from the mine entrance about 10 o'clock the morning of February 27, 1943, was the first indication of trouble. "There's something wrong down here. I'm getting out," the hoist operator called up. He and two nearby miners were the last men to leave the mine alive.

Rescue crews from as far away as Butte and Cascade County worked around the clock in six hour shifts to clear debris and search for possible survivors. There were none. The night of March 4, workers reached the first bodies. More followed until the toll mounted to 74. Some died as a result of a violent explosion in No. 3 vein, the remainder fell victim to the deadly methane gasses released by the blast.

The tragedy at Smith Mine became Montana's worst coal mine disaster, sparking investigations at the state and national level. Montana Governor Sam C. Ford visited the scene, offered state assistance and pushed a thorough inquiry into the incident.

Today's marker of the Smith Mine Disaster follows a simpler one left by two of the miners trapped underground after the explosions waiting for the poisonous gas they knew would come.

> "Walter & Johnny. Good-bye.
> Wives and Daughters We died an easy death. Love from us, both.
> Be good."

I consider the Smith Mine Disaster message well-written with most of the elements of interpretive writing. My assessment is that it would be better if it had a developed theme connected to a single goal. The goal might be a memorial to those lost, a statement of the dangers of mining, a tribute to the governor and the political process, or the telling of a story. All four of these possible goals are present. A singular goal would guide the direction of an identifiable theme, breaking the way for a strong interpretive message.

Exhibits Plan Example
The following is an excerpt from the first draft of a plan for an ocelot exhibit at the Oregon Zoo in Portland. The draft is credited to Charis Henrie with contributions from Anne Warner. The exhibit plan demonstrates how a team composed of a planner, writer, and designer collaborated on the project.

Ocelot Interpretive Plan
Major Message: Ocelots depend on trees to survive. Humans are helping ocelots and the trees they depend on.

Location #4 (Planter Bed across from exhibit)
Headline: More Trees for Ocelots

Text: With the help of the Brazilian Ocelot Consortium, ranchers around the Serra do Japi Biosphere Reserve in Brazil are working to reconnect patches of forests.

Once the connections are complete over 200 ocelots and hundreds of other species will be able to freely roam over a large area.

Sidebar Text: The Oregon Zoo is an active member of the Brazilian Ocelot Consortium. Funds we give to the consortium help pay for habitat restoration, environmental education, and training of Brazilian zoo keepers and scientists.

Photograph/Illustration Ideas:
* seedling nursery
* field of planted seedlings
* line of trees showing difference between reserve & unprotected space

Photo Captions:
* Local students raise native trees at their school.
* Neighbors plant seedlings around the reserve.

Location #5 (Wing Wall)
Headline: Ocelots Need Trees

Text: Ocelots live in many different habitats, from Texas and Arizona south to Argentina. From desert to mountain forests, the one feature these habitats have in common is thick plant cover.

Photograph/Illustration Ideas: Photo collage of ocelots in a variety of habitats—captions can be where the photo was taken (illustrate the range from Texas to Argentina (i.e. Amazon forest, Brazil, Sonora Desert, Mexico, Cloud Forest, Costa Rica etc…).

Sidebar Text: The last remaining ocelots in the United States are found in Texas and Arizona. Ocelots in these states move across the border with Mexico.

This example of an exhibit plan shows that the interpretive text is driven by a theme and focuses on a purpose. The theme and purpose are expressed in the major message. The text exclusively addresses the theme, the designer helped define the syntax by assigning sidebars, photo captions, and headlines. This is a good example of a collaborative team effort.

Developing Your Message

Before you begin a writing project, you must answer several developmental questions. It is important to answer these questions so that the expectations of you, the writer, are clear. Answer the questions in order.

1. What is the goal of interpreting the resource, object, relic, or concept?

2. How does the resource fit into a bigger story? For instance, if it is an object in a museum, how does it relate to the theme of the museum exhibit?

3. What universal concept do you want your audience to be aware of regarding the resource? Consider a big idea to attach to the resource.

4. What are the important tangible features of the resource? Describe the important physical attributes of the resource.

5. What are the intangible attributes of the resource? Consider how your audience perceives the resource. Think of what it means to them. They may have little or no attachment to the resource and feel neutral towards it. You need to be aware of what they know and their feelings about the resource.

6. What intellectual connections can you make regarding the resource? Review what your audience knows about things similar to the resource and plan to make connections.

7.   What emotional connections can you make regarding the resource? Consider how you can provide your audience with knowledge that is attached to an emotion.

8.   What higher-level final product are you moving your audience toward? Consider what you want your audience to be able to do, think, or feel as a result of reading your interpretive message.

9.   What theme statement do you want to develop? Write a theme state. Refine the theme statement by writing it five more times. Select the best theme statement to follow when writing your first draft.

10. How will the final product appear? Find out in what media form your writing will appear and who will be doing the design work.

Answering these 10 questions is crucial before beginning your writing. You can find the answers to these questions by discussing the goal of the writing with the project planners and visualizing how the final product will appear with the project designers. A team of the writer, the project planner, and the project designer accomplishes an effective interpretive writing project. Together you work toward the project goal.

MEDIA VARIATIONS

A trail guide, a postcard, a self-guided brochure, a news release, wayside signage, and a book review are some of the communication forms that interpretive writers use. The next five examples are samples of how interpretation of the red squirrel might appear in different media forms. An information-management sign follows the red squirrel examples. Finally, a book review of *The Last Season* that appeared in *The Interpreter* magazine completes the chapter. After each example, I have identified its interpretive writing elements. Remember, each message does not need to have all five elements of interpretive writing.

Trail Guide

Red squirrel

The red squirrel species inhabits the forests of the Seeley-Swan Valley. Locally known as the pine squirrel, these tree acrobats will delight you with their endearing antics.

You may detect pine squirrels by sight or sound. Their noisy chattering is a territorial cry. With a home range of less than two football fields and populations of two squirrels to three acres, their territories easily overlap. They do not like that and fight to protect their food. Red squirrels do not hibernate, and can live 10 years if they elude owls, martens, foxes, and bobcats.

Tangible(s): red squirrel, chattering, home range, food, and predators
Intangible(s): delight, endearing antics

Universal(s): territory

Emotional/Intellectual Connection: Chattering is a territorial cry to protect food.

Stewardship Component: N/A

Does the writing encourage the reader to want to learn more? Yes, through observation.

Flesch-Kincaid Reading Level: 7.7 grade, 93 words

Postcard

Red Squirrel
(Tamiasciurus hudsonicus)

Regardless of the season, you are never alone in the forest as long as you are in the range of the red squirrel. Active throughout the year, the red squirrel will tunnel beneath the snow to find food. Like you, red squirrels eat a wide variety of food, including, mushrooms, nuts, eggs, and seeds.

Tangible(s): red squirrel, forest, snow, the list of food squirrels eat

Intangible(s): you are never alone, range of the squirrel, like you

Universal(s): food

Emotional/Intellectual Connection: tunneling beneath snow for food, they eat similar foods to humans

Stewardship Component: N/A

Does the writing encourage the reader to want to learn more? No.

Flesch-Kincaid Reading Level: 7.1 grade, 54 words

Self-guided Trail Brochure

Listen for the chatter of this smallest squirrel forest dweller. A comical forest acrobat, the red squirrel is distinguished by its small size, reddish back, white belly, and white-eye patch. You might think it is fussing over your presence near its home. Instead, it is probably informing its neighbors of its whereabouts and warning them to stay away.

Tangible(s): red squirrel, chatter, home, neighboring squirrels

Intangible(s): fussing over your presence

Universal(s): home, warning
Emotional/Intellectual Connection: "It's not about you."
Stewardship Component: N/A
Does the writing encourage the reader to want to learn more? No.
Flesch-Kincaid Reading Level: 5.5 grade, 37 words

News Release

Parker Nature Center is celebrating springtime with a week of programs about one of its most common residents, red squirrels. Come and enjoy the festivities, free and open to the public beginning Saturday, March 21. Beginning at 10 AM a family walk through the forest will help you identify these playful animals and locate where they live. Additional activities include a nesting box building workshop, and an evening with Professor Piney La Squirrel. A complete schedule of events is available on the center's Web site, www.parkernc.com, or by calling 754-3809.

Tangible(s): red squirrel, nature center, springtime, programs, festivities, workshop, Professor Piney La Squirrel, events
Intangible(s): family involvement, joy of observation
Universal(s): celebration
Emotional/Intellectual Connection: learning about a neighbor animal
Stewardship Component: building nesting boxes
Does the writing encourage the reader to want to learn more? Yes, it promotes the reader's involvement.
Flesch-Kincaid Reading Level: 12.0 grade, 89 words

Wayside Sign

The Round Valley Scenic Byway has many treasures for you to explore. The ratchet-like chattering and acrobatic antics of the red squirrel may entertain you when you stop at the wayside exhibits. This tree squirrel is common in the byway environment and serves as an ambassador welcoming you along your journey.

Tangible(s): red squirrel, scenic byway, chattering, and exhibits
Intangible(s): treasures, exploration
Universal(s): welcoming
Emotional/Intellectual Connection: chattering and antics entertain
Stewardship Component: N/A

Does the writing encourage the reader to want to learn more? No.
Flesch-Kincaid Reading Level: 10.5 grade, 51 words

Posted Information Signage

Management signage written in positive, proactive language attracts readers. This
sign, posted at several lakes in Montana, engages readers on several levels: it is
visually interesting, it tells a story, it has a positive language, and it illustrates
validity through multi-agency support.

Tangible(s): loon, Montana, chicks, nest, eggs, parents

Intangible(s): magnificent bird, laughing matter, cry of the loon

Universal(s): responsibility, death, predators

Emotional/Intellectual Connection: the relationship between the facts about
    disturbing a loon and death of the young

Stewardship Component: You can help!

Does the writing encourage the reader to want to learn more? Maybe. It is
    intended as a management message, not to get readers to investigate further.

Flesch-Kincaid Reading Level: 5.0 grade, 129 words

Book Review

Larry Beck is the review editor for *The Interpreter* and is a professor of
environmental interpretation at San Diego State University. He wrote this book
review of Eric Blehm's *The Last Season* that appeared in the May/June 2006 issue
of *The Interpreter*. With Larry's permission, I have included it in this book as a
good example of an interpretive book review. A conventional approach to book
reviews is to talk about what appears in each chapter: "In chapter one, the author
says; chapter two deals with...." Instead, notice how Larry begins with a story. The
story becomes a testimonial that connects with you, the reader.

The Last Season by Eric Blehm

I was curious about *The Last Season* before it was even released in April
2006. A former student notified me and suggested I look at the Web site
for the book—thelastseason.com—to check it out. Here I found the
author researched the story over the course of eight years. Featured
reviews of the book were appearing in several major magazines. The book
had been endorsed by acclaimed writers such as Bill McKibben (*The End
of Nature*) who wrote, "This is a first-rate detective story, but it is an even
better love story—an account of the love for wild places that animates
some of us, leads us ever deeper in and higher up." All of the evidence
stacked up in favor of the book and I couldn't wait to read it, because, last
of all, that former student who alerted me to the book had written it.

In July 1996 a legendary backcountry ranger at Kings Canyon
National Park went on patrol and disappeared. *The Last Season* is the
story of Randy Morgenson, his life and death, and the ultimately
abandoned search and rescue effort that was launched to find him. The
tale is woven with elements of beauty and tragedy. Morgenson grew up
in Yosemite and was mentored by the likes of photographer Ansel
Adams and writer Wallace Stegner. He spent more time exploring the
High Sierra than John Muir. Yet in his later years he became troubled
(guilt-ridden, vulnerable, self-absorbed) for reasons that are disclosed in
the book. After 28 seasons in the backcountry, was he suicidal? Did he
find a place to take his life where he knew he would never be found?

Did he disappear to find a new life elsewhere? Was he murdered? Or was his death an accident?

Eric Blehm's tale reads like a mystery novel. But there is much more to it. This is the story of a man's love for a place that he knew like few others. Morgenson had a passion for Kings Canyon; everything about it. He was enchanted by the sights and sounds of this wonderland from the towering spires to the tiniest wildflowers. And he was able to convey this magic—his knowledge, his passion, his experiences—to others.

Years ago Barry Lopez told me that he was always intrigued when readers would remark that although he had written about "Subject A," they were inspired to consider "Subject B." In other words, Lopez had created an atmosphere in which readers could respond individually. Similarly, a current thrust in interpretation is to provide a forum for the audience to react to and build upon. The audience may consider new possibilities related to the story and create *personal* responses. Ideally the audience is provoked to *think* and to consider the material in the context of their own experiences. This is exactly what *The Last Season* offers to someone who has a passion for the land.

The backdrop of the drama is one of the most beautiful natural areas on the face of the planet. In reading Blehm's book I recalled a solo backpack in Kings Canyon just a year before Morgenson disappeared and just south of his patrol cabin that year. I was also prompted to consider those things that make other landscapes special—for me, some extraordinary places I've been privileged to work, such as Denali National Park and Preserve in Alaska. The backcountry tenor of Morgenson's work took me even further back to when I served as a wilderness ranger patrolling the San Juan River in Utah. I could relate to Morgenson's sense of proprietorship since no one else is closer to the land and has the opportunity to spend so much time there. And this is only the beginning of my response to *The Last Season*.

Where this book will take you I can't imagine. But my guess is that it will take you far beyond the mountains of the High Sierra. That's what good interpretation does. It employs universal concepts that everyone can relate to in the creation of *personal* meanings. As this story unfolds, the author employs many universal concepts such as beauty, freedom, mystery, family, and love. Ultimately the story is about life and death— and what it means to live. I highly recommend *The Last Season* and I would be interested in *your* response to the book.

Tangible(s): the book itself
Intangible(s): Larry talks about how he, an interpreter, relates to the book.
Universal(s): beauty, freedom, mystery, family, love, life, and death

Emotional/Intellectual Connection: Larry talks about his experiences and then
    makes an emotional connection to the book content.
Stewardship Component: None intended
Does the writing encourage the reader to want to learn more? Yes. The purpose of
    the review is to encourage you to read the book.
Flesch-Kincaid Reading Level: 8.5 grade, 767 words

This chapter provides you with examples of how interpretive writing elements can
appear in various media. Five examples are about the same resource, the red
squirrel. The other two are from a book review and management signage.
Collectively, they illustrate that interpretive writing elements are found in many
different media forms.

TITLES AND LEADS IN INTERPRETIVE WRITING

Referring to companies like Enron, comedian Lewis Black stated that a business that cannot tell what it does in one simple sentence should be outlawed. There are good examples of companies that do not need a sentence because their names give direction of what they do (Ford Motor Company, Pepsi Cola Bottling Company, Bell Telephone Company). There are many companies with names that do not (Amazon, eBay, Dragonfly). One of my favorite vague business names is Arcata Transit Authority. What do you think they do? I asked one of the sales clerks why they selected the name and he said the owner was considering a name change. Too much time was spent answering telephone inquires about the bus schedule for a business that sells bicycles. Lewis Black's assertion applies to interpretive writing projects as well. The interpretive attempt should be outlawed if the direction of the interpretive message is not apparent in the title or in the lead.

Titles and leads are the first words readers see in interpretive copy. They should be explicit in their function, and often their function is informing the reader what to expect in the message. Vague titles and leads may be clever but have little to do with the goal of the interpretive message. Robert Louis Stevenson declared, "Don't write merely to be understood. Write so that you cannot possibly be misunderstood."

Titles in Interpretive Writing

Titles attract. They attract with a single word or several. They can be a complete sentence or a fragment. They can be the name of a site followed by a subtitle that describes the resource. They can be a theme statement or not. They must relate to the interpretive message communicated in the rest of the label, brochure, or sign. The titles in this sign (pictured on the following page) from Deanna DeChristopher and Folio Design leaves no doubt about the direction of the interpretive message.

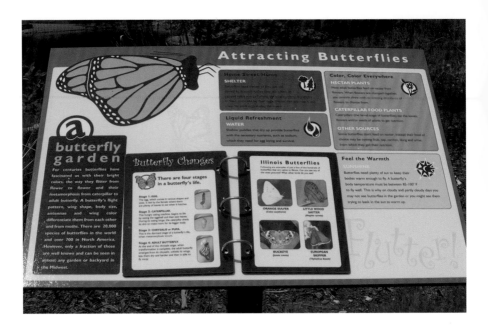

I have learned to resist the temptation to use clichés as titles ("Mother's Milk," "Flight of Fancy," "Time Marches On") in favor of titles that are descriptive with an action verb, such as this Bureau of Land Management brochure title for Garnet Ghost Town in Montana.

COME EXPLORE MONTANA'S EXCITING PAST!

| d into the Montana | This remote town boasted hotels, stores and | Today, most of the town |
| s. Homesteaders rode | saloons, as well as a school, laundry, drug store, | managed by the Bureau |

The verb should express the main "what" of the story and should be placed early in the title in order to attract attention. Explore is the "what" in the title above. There is one criterion for assessing the effectiveness of a title: Does it get the reader to read further?

Leads in Interpretive Writing

Interpretation is a process of telling a story, whether the interpretation is on a museum label, on a Web page, in a brochure, or in a newsletter article. Each story has the elements of a beginning, a body, and a conclusion. The elements of the story can appear as several museum labels, the various stops listed in a self-guided brochure, the different links to a Web page, or individual signs along a scenic byway. For instance, a set of 15 signs along a scenic byway makes up a story.

Every interpretive story begins with a lead. The lead may be the first stop along a scenic byway or the first paragraph of a self-guided brochure. The lead to

Attract readers with headlines that give a strong feeling. Note this article by John Gleeson of the Winnipeg Sun as reported in *The Week*, July 7–14, 2006, page16.

How not to attract tourists

Manitoba's new motto "is, in a word, 'Lame-o,'" said John Gleeson in the *Winnipeg Sun*. The province handed Over $600,000 to a marketing task force to come up with a new slogan to attract tourism, and in return we got this phrase: "Spirited energy." The first thing that struck me about the phrase is that it hardly rolls off the tongue. Try saying it three times fast and you just might choke to death. "The next thing I realized about the slogan is that it really sucks." Both "spirit" and "energy" are utterly vague. Put them together "and what you've got is mush."

What kind of energy doesn't have spirit? It's easy to see what the marketers were going for in focusing on energy; after all, Manitoba has vast hydroelectric potential. Yet surely there's a pithier way to reference our resources. The word "power," for example, has much more punch. How about, "Manitoba: Feel the power"? Instead, we're stuck with a motto obviously made by committee. The task force "would have done better throwing rocks at Portage and Main and asking the first person they hit for a winning slogan."

an interpretive story attracts the reader, informs the reader, and teaches the reader how to process the rest of the story. Every interpretive message begins with a lead, so learning to write a good lead is the first step in learning to write a good story. A reader is likely to spend only a few seconds deciding whether to follow an interpretive story, whether appearing in a magazine, set of museum labels, brochure, or byway signs. If the lead does not hold the reader's interest, the interpretive writer's efforts are in vain.

Regardless of the type of lead, keep it short. Short leads are more likely to capture a reader's interest. Even in a feature article, if your lead is over 65 words, it probably is too long. Your lead in a 12-panel byway sign project may be the first panel. Again, keep it short. Interpretive writers use different styles of leads, depending on the goal of the message, the media selected, and the audience.

I am going to identify and discuss 11 types of leads: the question, the announcement, the definition, the anecdote, the use of figurative language, the factual position, the quotation, the discordant statement, painting a picture, a personal experience story, and the technique of starting with an important observation.

The Question

Ask anyone a question and you will get some sort of response. People are attracted to questions. Make your lead an interesting question that relates to your theme. Anticipate the most important question your readers might have about the theme. Use it. In many ways, interpretation is about trying to answer visitors' most important questions. Learn your audiences' characteristics and ask the question to which they would want to know the answer, as Jenny Dyer did in this panel for the Denver Zoo.

WHY DO LIONS ROAR?

It's better than fighting. Listening lions can tell where roaring lions are located, how many there are, and if they're male or female. Keeping their distance helps rival lions avoid injury or even death.

Roaring also lets prowling pride members keep track of one another, call for help, or just call the whole crowd to dinner.

"Why do lions roar?" is a good, straight-forward question that will create a center of attention for any audience. Unusual questions have the same impact. Below, Denise Dahn shows the reader a convoluted question that gets everyone thinking.

Do salmon grow on trees?

Yes! They depend on fallen trees and on standing forests too. Forested headwaters are a major reason that Griffin Creek is such excellent salmon habitat.

Griffin Creek is one of the best coho spawning areas in Puget Sound. The creek also supports chinook, chum, and pink salmon, and cutthroat and steelhead trout.

You can't see them from here, but the headwaters of Griffin Creek lie mostly within private forestland. Sensitive logging practices can produce timber and provide wildlife habitat.

The Announcement

Heralding a declaration heightens people's attention. Begin with a leading statement about the theme that will follow. Do not start with "I am going to tell you about...." Allow the reader to discern what the interpretive message is about. Below is a good example from a children's activity poster that the San Diego Zoo disseminated to patients at a local hospital.

MEET LOON - a baboon whose favorite food is broccoli!

Would you let the doctor give you a shot if he offered you broccoli as a reward? One of the baboons at the San Diego Zoo did! Loon was an 11-year-old drill, a type of baboon that is endangered. A few years ago, Loon lost a lot of weight even though he had been a big eater. The Zoo's vets learned that Loon had a disease called diabetes. Diabetes kept Loon's body from converting sugar into energy. Loon needed daily insulin shots, just like humans who have diabetes. But how do you give a shot to a 33 - 50 pound primate with 3" canine teeth? The Zoo's staff decided to train Loon to get his shot of insulin. They did this by offering him food rewards. Loon especially loved mealworms and broccoli!

The Definition

Have you ever consulted a dictionary about a word and found yourself thumbing through the book looking up others? We like to know the meaning of things. Open with a definition of the concept you are interpreting. The definition can be your own or come from a dictionary or textbook. If you take it from a dictionary or recognized agency, be sure to use quotation marks and give credit to the source.

Mary Lou Herlihy of the National Park Service, Oakland, California, contributes the following example. The text is from the Devil's Orchard panel series at Craters of the Moon National Monument and Preserve in Idaho.

It's in the Air

The colorful little patches on the rock in front of you are lichens. First plants to grow in the "orchard," they slowly dissolve rock into soil, where more advanced plants can take root.

Tough as they are, lichens can still be threatened by human activity because they store airborne chemicals in their cells. Microscopic examinations show that lichens at Craters of the Moon have been damaged by polluted air. First to grow and first to be damaged, lichens warn us that the park's air suffers from polluters near and far.

Quote: As crude a weapon as the cave man's club, the chemical barrage has been hurled against the fabric of life. Rachel Carson

Image: close up view of colorful lichens.

The Anecdote

Interpreters are story-tellers for a reason: because people like to find understanding through narratives. Consider beginning your interpretive text with a short account of an event. Mary Lou Herlihy provides another example from the Devil's Orchard panel series to illustrate the anecdote.

Good Neighbors

A hundred years ago the minister looked at grotesque rocks and twisted trees here, and saw only a "garden fit for a devil." Today we look at the same scene and see a geological laboratory, a resource fit for the scientist, the hiker, the curious visitor. A hundred years from now, for whom who will the Devil's Orchard be fit for?

The answer has less to do with volcanoes than it has to do with all of us.

Use Figurative Language

Symbolic language provides abstractions that adults find mentally challenging and entertaining. Begin your message with a metaphor (a contrast of two objects implicitly saying one thing is another thing), a simile (a type of metaphor that is an assessment of two things using the words, *like, as,* or *is*), or a personification (giving human qualities to something nonhuman). All figurative messages are fun to craft, but keep in mind they must relate to your theme.

Metaphors make a comparison between two dissimilar things. Gene Ervine of the Alaska Office of the Bureau of Land Management offers this panel title as a metaphor: "Spring: A Leap Into Life." The metaphor is spring being a leap. I have included the first paragraph of the text and an image of the panel in which it appears.

Spring: A Leap Into Life

In a land desperate for change, the returning sunlight brings dramatic rebirth to the arctic. As the northern regions point more and more toward the sun, the returning daylight brings an explosion of life to the region.

I have challenged participants in my writing workshops to give examples of metaphors. Most of their examples are similes, metaphors that use *like, as,* or *is*. They are easier to craft than a non-simile metaphor. If the previous example were written as a simile it would read, "Spring *is Like* a Leap Into Life." Denise Dahn of Dahn Design, LLC provides this example of a simile from a project for Oregon State Parks. The simile is "Northwest rivers were like...."

The third form of figurative language irritates some science professionals. Ascribing human characteristics to animals or inanimate objects can minimize the complex role they have in nature. Used with discretion, personification is a powerful way to connect with your audiences. Gene Ervine contributes this example from a panel about black bears. Again, I have chosen to show only the salient parts of the text.

See Chapter 11, "Figures of Speech," for more on metaphors, similes, and personification.

Black Bears – Ambling Food Factories

With a teenager's enthusiasm for food, black bears eat tons of berries, fresh meat, grasses, carrion or camper's food to fatten themselves for their winter rest.

Black Bears – Ambling Food Factories

With a teenager's enthusiasm for food, black bears eat tons of berries, fresh meat, grasses, carrion or camper's food to fatten themselves for their winter rest.

Curious and focused on eating, these bears often surprise humans, or are surprised themselves. It is essential to keep a clean camp in bear country or your supplies may supplement a bear's winter stores.

Living on stored fat, black bears become dormant in winter. During this long nap they remain semi-alert, and females give birth and care for their young.

Black Bear Facts

- **Weight:** 180 to 250 lbs.
- **Height (at shoulder):** 26 to 36 in.
- **Length (with tail):** $4^{1}/_{2}$ to $5^{1}/_{2}$ ft.
- **Habits:** solitary; semi-hibernators
- **Home Range:** 10 to 40 sq. mi.
- Pelt with long guard hairs is comm(used for rugs.

The Factual Position

Every agency, site, or organization has a fundamental premise on which it is established. Start your story with your agency's position about the principle. This is similar to a bold and challenging statement, but you let the reader know whose opinion it is right away. The interpretive message of The Negro Leagues Baseball Museum's brochure starts:

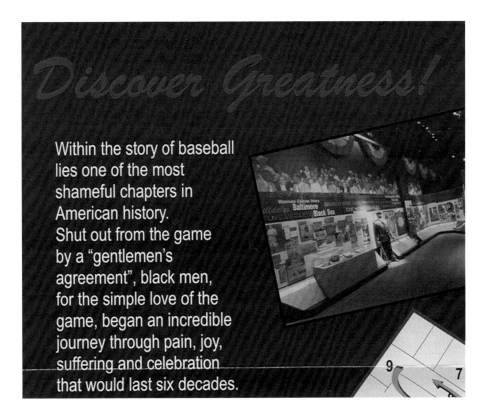

Within the story of baseball lies one of the most shameful chapters in American history. Shut out from the game by a "gentlemen's agreement", black men, for the simple love of the game, began an incredible journey through pain, joy, suffering and celebration that would last six decades.

Quotation from a Recognizable Source

James Stewart's character in the motion picture Western classic *Destry Rides Again* finds that quoting supposed authority figures gets people's initial and lasting attention. Quoting actual and recognizable authorities or famous people can do the same for you, but there are some cautions. As I noted earlier, avoid clichéd and overused passages. Some famous people have been over-cited. Use special care when selecting quotations from John Muir, Aldo Leopold, Ralph Waldo Emerson, and Henry David Thoreau. Make sure the excerpt relates to your theme and not just a quotation to establish an emotion in an obtrusive manner.

Is it advisable to quote political figures? Many political figures have molded our culture. People like George Washington, Abraham Lincoln, and Thomas Jefferson have contributed to our worldview. The contributions of more recent political figures remains debatable. Readers often disagree about the credibility of a quotation. There is, for example, polarization among peoples' feelings of the contributions of Franklin Roosevelt to conservation. Interpretive writers want to attract readers. Avoid any quotation that might elicit an emotional response that detracts from achieving your goal.

I learned in high school that if I wanted to have an enjoyable time with new acquaintances, I avoided political and religious conversations. Interpretive writers should do the same, (unless the goal of the message is political or religious). People have intransigent feelings about both. These feelings are associated with cultural values that are often indescribable, rooted in complex interactions of family, personal experience, and faith-based practices. Interpretive messages that use faith-based quotations can distract from your interpretive goal. Quotations that do not target the theme launch the reader in the wrong direction. Society remains divided on whether it is appropriate to display sectarian messages on public property. Stay away from quoting the Bible or the Koran—unless the passage leads to meeting your goal. Otherwise, there is no reason to risk turning readers away.

Quotations are strong attractants if the quote is from an authority or a famous person and the quote is short. The following is a good example of how a quotation introduces the theme and attracts the reader. Caryn Davidson from Joshua Tree National Park contributes this short quotation from a familiar source as it appears in a site bulletin.

Elemental Things: Air Quality in Joshua Tree National Park

It is only with the heart that one can see rightly. What is essential is invisible to the eyes.

~ *The Little Prince*, by Antoine de Saint-Exupéry

Many visitors are drawn to Joshua Tree National Park because they ozone molecules to every ten million molecules of air. When the number throughout the park has been impaired due to poor air quality. You can see the current view from Belle Mountain looking southeast, via a webcam, at www.nps.gov/jotr. Look for the "weather webcam" link on the left side of the home page.

The Discordant Statement

A creative and fun way to get your readers' attention is to get them "off balance" with a mentally dissonant claim. Make an assertion that does not connect. Discordant allegations attract readers. They want to know more in order to feel mental balance. Here is another site bulletin example from Joshua Tree National Park.

Cheaters Sometimes Prosper:
Exotic Grasses in Joshua Tree National Park

The Problem: The fire regime in Joshua Tree National Park...

Paint a Picture

This is an opportunity for you to be playful, and use what Freeman Tilden referred to as "the light touch." Use expressive and colorful language to build an image for your readers. The following is an example from an article called "Expatriates Bar & Grill: Fine Food, Cigars, and Environmental Espionage" written by Jon Kohl.

While it may look like just another pretty bar with a burly blue-eyed Canadian distributing beers, Expatriates Bar & Grill harbors the deal-making subterfuge of Geneva, Berlin, or Cairo. But the figures haunting these halls are not so dark, nor are they spies. They are likely members of the international development and business communities in La Ceiba, Honduras.

Personal Experience

Your lead can be a story. It can be a story about a famous person or someone who has encountered your resource. The lead can also be from your personal experience. The following is a lead I used in my editorial in the May/June 2006 issue of *The Interpreter* magazine. The lead is an interaction I had with my father.

"Diversity"
It must have been in July, when I was home from college, that my father asked me to help him with the central air-conditioning unit. It needed a new filter and cleaning. He studied the outside of the trunk-like metal box and observing that tools were needed to gain access. He requested, "Go to the garage and get my tool box." I complied.

Start with an Important Observation

Put the most important observation or fact into the lead. Rangers at Yellowstone National Park entrance stations give out the following flyer. The lead is "SPEED KILLS."

Leads capture readers. If your lead does not capture your reader, your writing efforts have been in vain. Rewrite the lead until it works. Economist/author John Kenneth Galbraith declared that for him, the note of spontaneity detected in his writing did not appear until the fifth rewrite. Play with the words and the ideas. Notice that the examples I have given play with words. Become a student of how others write their leads, and mimic the ones you feel work.

CAPTURING YOUR
READER'S ATTENTION

Your ambition as an interpretive writer is to entice your audience to read your message and embrace your takeaway point. In order to do this you must create your message so that your audience wants to continue reading once they have begun. Capturing your reader also is known as hooking them. How do you accomplish capturing your reader?

A designer might declare that the font, its point size, appropriate layout enhanced by graphics, an attractive color scheme, and the positioning of the message are the initial determining factors whether audiences will read your copy. This is true. These elements are essential in attracting readers. Visualize advertising copy without imagery. Imagery is intended to capture the audience and complete the message by augmenting the copy. What techniques do interpretive writers use to draw the reader into the copy?

Whether the messages are written for a wayside panels, public service announcements, museum labels, brochures, feature articles, books, scripts, or other long pieces, interpretive writers select techniques that are engaging to an audience. Techniques of capturing your readers we have discussed are a second-person orientation, visualizations, creating mystery, developing mental dissonance, using a metaphor, including unusual facts, asking questions, using quotations, telling stories, using rich language, focusing on action verbs that evoke emotion, and using what Freeman Tilden called "the light touch."

Hooks appear any place within a paragraph. I ask my reviewers to make notations where they are distracted by noise. I then consider using a hook at this point to keep my readers engaged.

The following are examples of interpretive writing that capture readers with quotations, the light touch, mystery, a question, using a metaphor, pending storylines, and a second-person orientation.

Boardwalk Sign

Ever bathe in used *water*?
Of course! For millions of years,
life on earth has used and re-used
the same water!

All water on earth is constantly being recycled
as part of the global water cycle. The water
molecules in your bath may have one been in
George Washington's tea, Napoleon's hair tonic,
or a dinosaur's drink!

> *Starts with a question and uses the light touch.*
> (Corkscrew Swamp, Courtesy of Dahn Design)

Wayside Panel

When the rumble of trucks and cars fades into the distance, listen
to the silence.

Look around you at this open landscape that would be easily
identified by travelers from earlier eras.

Here, at the juncture of the Blackfoot and Seeley-Swan Valleys...

> *Challenges the senses.*
> (This sign is at a rest stop at the junction of Montana Highways 200 and 83.
> By Deborah Richie Oberbillig.)

Book

The house always had a strange smell, as though Daisy had found
some vegetable to boil that no one else knew about.

> *Use of humor (the light touch) and a pending storyline.*
> (*Montana 1948*, Larry Watson)

Wayside Panel

Oh! "Mama Sage." It seems endless, the sage: the rolling sage-covered Wyoming hills. Sagebrush, the shrub that means survival to the world's largest populations of pronghorn antelope and sage grouse.

Use of a metaphor.
(This sign is at a rest stop along Interstate 80 east of Rock Springs, Wyoming.)

Brochure

Rare Wildlife Oasis
UFO sightings may have put Roswell on the map, but at nearby Bitter Lake National Wildlife Refuge, strange creatures are more than visitors. They inhabit odd sinkholes, playa lakes, seeps and gypsum springs fed by an underground river.

At first glance, you might pinpoint the wintering 10,000 sandhill cranes and 20,000 snow geese as the refuge superlatives. Take a deeper look. Where the Chihuahuan Desert meets the Southern Plains, bizarre geology is responsible for habitats supporting wildlife you'll find nowhere else in the world.

Makes a comparison.
(Bitter Lake National Wildlife Refuge, New Mexico.
By Deborah Richie Oberbillig.)

Signage

You Are Invited To Participate!

Did you know that according to the U.S. Environmental Protection Agency, only 3% of the Earth's water is fresh?

In an effort to conserve water and energy, and to minimize the release of detergents into the environment, we invite you to participate in our environmental campaign.

A towel on the floor says. "Please replace."
A towel hung up says, "I'll use it again."

Thank you for helping protect our Environment!

Uses second-person orientation.
(Notice posted in a Maine hotel bathroom.)

Magazine Article

Chicago Wilderness magazine provides good examples of how to capture readers (see the image on the opposite page). The title is attractive. The first paragraph is a one-sentence question, a classic hook. The second paragraph asks you to relate to the resource as if you were a specialized scientist. The third paragraph challenges you to look at the photograph from a different perspective. The fifth paragraph hooks the reader with dissonance, "A natural forest wouldn't look like that." The last paragraph gives a personal reflection about the subject of the photograph. The article hooks you from title to conclusion, fulfilling an ambition of interpretive writers, getting you to read the entire text.

Reading pictures

Black and Light

If you were a buck, wouldn't you just love this sleek doe, her wet black nose, those ears so delicate the morning sun shines through them?

If you were a botanist, you'd probably focus on the ancient prairie in the foreground. Rattlesnake master, lead plant, and the wide leaves of prairie dock. Weedier and ranker, big bluestem grass and tall coreopsis show up nearer the edge, where the brush and trees have been cut back.

But look at this scene through the eyes of a conservationist. It's amazing that such complexity as is here can also show so much black and white.

The bottom of the photo is predominantly white from the sparkle of the dew. The top is mostly black, because neither the camera nor your eye can see much there—in the dense shade of the plague of shrubs and trees that have invaded this original prairie.

A natural forest wouldn't look like that. In this case we have a few species of invasive trees but none of the native shrubs, wildflowers, grasses, birds, or butterflies of an open, light-filled, natural forest. The black that the camera sees is truly representative of what the ecologist finds.

Some people would call the black background here a "forest" and complain if it were cut down. I appreciate their feelings. But increasing numbers of people see the pushing back of these invasive species as a small loss for a great gain. People who care for nature are becoming more and more informed, by taking field classes, helping with habitat restoration, and reading about how ecology works. They want to be part of the work to expand the edges of our pathetically few ancient prairies, savannas, and oak woodlands. They want to see beyond black and white— to a world of colors, and wondrous complexity.

Photo by Carol Freeman. Somme Prairie Grove is protected and managed by the Forest Preserve District of Cook County. Much of the brush clearing is done by the intrepid volunteers of the North Branch Restoration Project. Words by Stephen Packard.

SHOW, RATHER
THAN TELL

Read this, then close your eyes and follow the instructions. Hold your right hand 12 inches from your mouth. Picture holding in your hand a fresh, ripe lemon. It is the size of your fist; notice its weight. Turn the lemon over feel its uneven surface. Feel its cool skin. Think about biting through its skin.

My mouth waters every time I give these instructions. The instructions provide powerful images of something visualized by those of us who have ever bitten into a piece of lemon. Visualizations (imagery) lay out the scene as the eye sees it, with emphasis and emotion in unlikely places. If I write, "The river is stunning and powerful," I am telling. But if I write, "I am stunned by the river's unabated rampage as it rushes through the canyon—foaming cascades, thunderous to my ear," I am showing. The moment the reader can visualize the picture I am trying to paint, I am showing, rather than telling what the reader should visualize.

Granted, context is everything, as writing experts say. If the resource, object, relic, or artifact is displayed, there is little need to show. If it is not available, then interpreting it through the senses is appropriate.

Draw upon words that provide imagery that open up or describe in specifics what is unique about the person, place, or event being interpreted. Avoid words like handsome, attractive, momentous, embarrassing, fabulous, powerful, hilarious, stupid, and fascinating. They are words that "tell" an arbitrary way to think. They are often prefaced with clichés and do not reveal meanings.

The difference between showing and telling resides in challenging the physical senses. Visual, tactile, aural, aromatic words connect us to the resource being interpreted. Note how interpretation specialist Russell Virgilio's description of Bumpass Hell in the May–November 2006 issue Lassen Volcanic National Park's "Peak Experiences" shows the reader the resource.

Imagine you are standing on the boardwalk at Bumpass Hell. You can feel the light earthquake-like shaking of active hydrothermal features below.

You close your eyes as the sounds of hissing fumaroles, boiling springs, and gurgling mud pots are interrupted only by the rotten egg smell of drifting sulphur clouds. After a morning hike to Bumpass Hell, you decide to have lunch beneath Lassen Peak along the shores of Lake Helen. A sudden gust of wind brings a sense of peace and quiet as the mirror image reflection of Lassen Peak ripples in the waves. Lassen Volcanic National Park bears many gifts just waiting to be received by all who visit.

Deanna DeChristopher of Chicago contributed this panel as an example of how interpretive writers can challenge the senses.

The following is an example of creating imagery with the assistance of a graphic designer, courtesy of Idaho State Parks.

Gene Ervine, interpretive writer for the Bureau of Land Management, Alaska State Office provides this example how a narrative becomes visual and active with the selection of dynamic verbs. You do not need graphics to capture the imagery.

Second Draft
Signage at Finger Rock Wayside, Dalton Highway

A Rock...and A Hard Place

Finger Rock and the other granite tors that dot this landscape speak of the old days, the real old days when magma squirted through racks in rock. Cooling lava formed a tough granite, harder than the surrounding rock. The harsh climate of this place wore away the softer stone, leaving the granite above the surrounding landscape.

Water worked its way into cracks in the rock around the granite. The Arctic cold turned the water into wedges of ice that split the rocks apart, leaving the granite tors, enduring monuments in a hard place. Look for evidence of this process as you visit.

Challenge your readers with words that arouse imagery

Taste...   Feel...   Listen...   Pretend...
Smell...   Hear...   Imagine...   Think of...

FIGURES OF SPEECH

Figures of speech help interpretive writing make connections. Analogies, comparisons, metaphors, similes, and personifications can connect readers to heritage resources in exciting, creative ways.

Analogies

An analogy shows a similarity between two things in order to make one of the things easier to understand. One of the things is familiar to the reader and is called the referent. Note that I have highlighted the salient words and phrases in the following examples.

> Rain, wind, rockslides caused by freezing and thawing, and the grinding of today's glaciers result in erosion that wears down the mountains at the rate of about one inch (2.5 centimeters) per year. *That is about as much as your fingernails grow annually.*
>
> —*Going to Glacier*, Alan Leftridge

Annual growth of the reader's fingernails is the referent to understanding the rate of erosion by glaciers.

The following is an example from Idaho State Parks of a tree stump analogous to a bed and breakfast inn.

Here, *a dead tree* is analogous to *a bed and breakfast inn.*

Comparisons

Whereas analogies compare a familiar thing to something that is similar but unfamiliar, comparisons examine two or more things to discover differences as well as similarities. For instance, I can make a comparison between the American flag and the Chilean flag. They are similar because they are both red, white, and blue, and rectangular. They are different because the Chilean flag has one white star, the American 50, and the American flag has 13 stripes to Chilean flag's two.

Interpretive writer Faye Goolrick offers these comparisons from a United States Fish and Wildlife Service exhibit at the Okefenokee National Wildlife Refuge. Notice how Faye uses the word *like* in both texts. This categorizes the texts as the form of metaphor known as a simile. She illustrates how figures of speech often overlap.

[Wall panel accompanying four-foot-high "glass of iced tea" illustrating "black water" concept of cypress swamp]

Swamp Tea

Okefenokee water is clean and clear—but it's permanently stained to the color of iced tea. Like household tea, the swamp's water becomes light brown from steeping in organic matter that gives off tannic acid. In the Okefenokee, the "tea leaves" are a complex brew of decaying vegetation.

[Interactive: Insert hand in "feel the peat" hole]

Feel the Peat... If You Dare!

What does peat feel like? Hmm. Squishy, but not slimy. Like fine-grained dirt, but not sandy. Like sticking your hand into cotton candy, but without the stickiness or the finger-licking sweetness. Peat is the name for decomposed remains of organic matter. So....
It feels like....it used to be....ALIVE!!!

Metaphors

The ancient Greeks used the word metaphor to mean "carry something across" or "transfer." Aristotle referred to the concept as giving a thing a name that belongs to something else. Diomedes called the metaphor "the transferring of things and words from their proper signification to an improper similitude for the sake of beauty, necessity, polish, or emphasis."

Today, a metaphor is a figure of speech that is intended to symbolize, compare, and paint an image. A metaphor underscores a likeness between two objects without using the words *like, as,* or *is*. Examples are "Your eyes are diamonds," "You are the world to me," and "His blood froze." You can enrich your interpretive writing by expressing the essence of an artifact or resource in terms of something that seems unrelated.

Metaphors enliven ordinary language. Interpretive writers have the power to make the ordinary strange and the strange ordinary, making life more interesting. The following are examples from Judy Fort Brenneman:

Peregrines are hard to spot.
You might see one knifing through the air in a spectacular dive, spy a courtship flight in early April, or catch some fledglings learning to fly and hunt in late July.

Metaphorical language encourages interpretation. When readers encounter a phrase or word they cannot take literally, they must make their own meaning.

North Arm's High-Flying Highway
Look up!
Above you is one of the most important highways in the Western Hemisphere. It's a migration corridor formed by the Wasatch Mountains...

Metaphors are more efficient and economical than ordinary language; they give maximum meaning with a minimum of words.

Freshwater Paradise
The deep, cold, clear water of Causey Reservoir teems with insects and invertebrate life—midges and caddisflies, zooplankton and algae, crayfish and snails.

Metaphors and humor make a good combination. The Great Eyeball Race by Jon Kohl appeared in the November/December 2004 issue of *The Interpreter*. The following paragraph is a light-hearted metaphor.

As I peered out my office window, I saw those visiting eyeballs roll into the parking lot, bouncing and bumbling as they went. When they caught a glimpse of our front gate, designed as a castle, they got excited and rushed in. Upon entering, the eyes greeted the crocodiles and turtles.

They hovered and ogled for a bit and then noticed the jaguar and tapir cages to the left. The eyes hurried over, missing the small "interpretive" signs. Only moments later one eye spied monkeys, blinked to other eyes, and off they went. And in no time the eyeballs had raced around the small zoo before finally rolling out in the parking lot to disappear into the urban bowels.

Metaphors create new meanings. They allow you to write about feelings, thoughts, things and experiences. The following is an excerpt from a Negro Leagues Baseball Hall of Fame brochure.

> The Negro Leagues rose from the ashes of segregation to become one of the most significant chapters in American history.

Finally, note the metaphor of nature's stage in this concessionaire's brochure from Crater Lake National Park, Volcano Cruises.

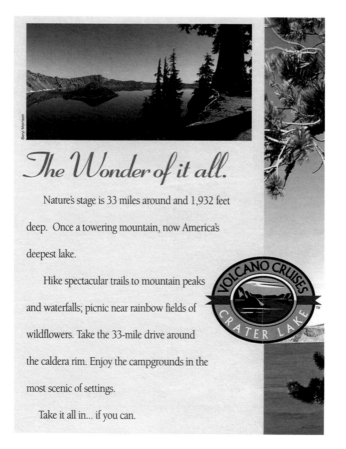

The Wonder of it all.

Nature's stage is 33 miles around and 1,932 feet deep. Once a towering mountain, now America's deepest lake.

Hike spectacular trails to mountain peaks and waterfalls; picnic near rainbow fields of wildflowers. Take the 33-mile drive around the caldera rim. Enjoy the campgrounds in the most scenic of settings.

Take it all in... if you can.

Mixed Metaphors

Think twice about using mixed metaphors, which are an awkward, often silly use of more than one metaphor at a time. Mixed metaphors are confusing and have no place in interpretive writing.

The campfire program struck a spark that massaged the visitor's conscience.

And, from Lee Cooke, mayor, Austin, Texas:

I want to have all my ducks in a row so that if we did get into a posture we could pretty much slam-dunk this thing and put it to bed.

Or this example from an article in the *Des Moines Register*:

I'm tired of being Charlie Brown and putting in more hoops for teachers to jump through and then pulling the football of higher salaries away at every turn.

Similes

Similes are a type of metaphor. Examples of similes include: "When Ron saw the bear his face became pale as the moon." "The ship's sails are smooth as silk." And "Locating a Luna moth on a day like today is like trying to find a needle in a haystack."

The following simile examples are introductory sentences of longer interpretive texts. Deirdre Ballou of the San Diego Zoo contributed this simile, which is part of an exhibit at the zoo.

Interpretive Journal

Like animals, epiphytic orchids depend on the forest trees, and as forests are cut down, there is nowhere for them to survive. People love orchids because they're beautiful—let's hope that love extends to protecting their native habitat as well.

Another simile example comes from Gene Ervine of the Alaska office of the Bureau of Land Management.

Lynx

Silent as drifting smoke on huge feet resembling furry floor mops, these keen eyed, night hunting cats feed on snowshoe hares and other small mammals.

Finally, Judy Fort Brenneman contributes this simile about eagle feathers and cat whiskers.

> Tiny feathers near the base of the eagle's bill and around its eyes provide sensory information, *like the whiskers on a cat.*

Personification

Giving human attributes or traits to non-human objects is called personification. Examples of personifications are "The angry clouds shed their tears" and "The trees danced in the wind before the rain fell."

Notice in this example from Idaho State Parks, that the tree stump is talking.

Finally, notice the use of personification and simile in Fort Brenneman's *Legacy* magazine essay:

> Eventually the bear heads back across the river, walking majestically— until one of his front paws slips off a stepping stone and *plop! splash!* plunges into the cold water. His paw is soaked; he looks *like a king* who's stepped in a mudhole. The family, ordinary folks, gape in surprise and hold their breath, knowing the king's reaction could go either way— heads have rolled for less – but today, the bear shakes his paw deliberately, sighs, and looks back over his shoulder as if to say, "Well, what can you do?" He shifts his shoulders as if settling royal robes into place and, head

held high enough to be elegant but not so high as to be arrogant,
continues confidently across the river and disappears into the brush.

Interpretive writers use personifications, similes, metaphors, comparisons, and
analogies to connect unfamiliar resource attributes with language recognizable to
their audiences. These figures of speech provide opportunities to make new
information memorable.

ACTIVE VERBS

Interpreters enliven their writing with active (action) verbs. Verbs come in several forms, including words that do not express action (such as *is, became, was,* and *do*), nouns used as verbs (like *to program, enthuse,* and *beef up*), and words that state that an action is taking place. These are active verbs. Active verbs have vigor, are concrete, and they are easier to analyze than passive verbs and abstractions.

I learned to recognize active verbs in sentences by looking at every word and asking myself, "Is this something that a person or thing can do, as opposed to a state of being?"

Consider this simple example: "The people applauded Mary's campfire program." Can you people? No. Can you applaud? Yes. Can you campfire? No. Can you program? Is programming something you can do? Yes, when using a noun (programmer) as a verb.

Using these questions, I recognize an action verb when I see one.

"Jim Bridger lost his stirrup." Can Bridger lose a stirrup? Yes, *losing* is something that Bridger can do.

"The Swan River National Wildlife Refuge provides nesting habitat for the endangered bald eagle." *Providing* is something that the refuge can do.

"The Flathead Area is full of places to view wildflowers." *Viewing* is something that a visitor can do.

"The Montana Native Plant Society leads field trips and sponsors local activities to educate its membership on the values of Montana's native flora." The Society can *lead, sponsor,* and *educate*—each an action verb.

The following example shows how an action verb replaces a weak verb for dynamic impact:

> "The Libby Dam *is* 17 miles upstream from the town of Libby in the heart of beautiful northwestern Montana."

The verb *is* does not convey a strong image of the Libby Dam. The U.S. Army

Corps of Engineers authors, on the other hand, wrote the passage using the active verb, *spans*. This verb provides a more powerful image:

> "The Libby Dam spans the Kootenai River 17 miles upstream from the town of Libby in the heart of beautiful northwestern Montana."

How does a writer know to use an active verb such as *spans* rather than the weaker verb like *is*? The best way is to build a large vocabulary. Build a large vocabulary by reading. As Nobel Prize-winning novelist William Faulkner advised, "Read, read, read. Read everything—trash, classics, good and bad, and see how they do it. Just like a carpenter who works as an apprentice and studies the master."

To help remind me of strong action verbs to use in my writing, I have collected a list of several hundred in alphabetical order. Reviewing this list helps me select strong concrete words that enliven my interpretive writing. The following figure lists some of the active verbs used in this book.

Examples of Active Verbs

accelerate	encourage	nurture	secure
accomplish	examine	observe	show
acquire	facilitate	orchestrate	specify
advance	focus	originate	speculate
amplify	generate	pattern	stage
analyze	guide	persuade	submit
attract	host	preserve	support
broaden	identify	produce	synthesize
build	illustrate	prompt	target
capture	influence	pursue	transfer
challenge	introduce	quantify	transform
collect	involve	rank	travel
construct	join	reconcile	uncover
create	launch	reinforce	unify
define	maintain	replace	utilize
direct	merge	result	validate
distinguish	motivate	revamp	welcome
earn	narrate	revitalize	write

ACTIVE VOICE
AND PASSIVE VOICE

We frequently have a choice of whether a noun will be the subject or object of a sentence, with a resulting difference in the verb form. The great majority of sentences use active verbs but sometimes the passive is appropriate. The passive voice consists of a form of *be* plus the past participle (*is given, are chosen, was taken, have been*). Passive voice appears when the use of personal pronouns is uncommon as the subjects of sentences. Active voice, on the other hand, helps to create clear and direct sentences.

Active Voice
The subject performs the action expressed in the verb. A verb is active if the verb's subject did, is doing, or will do something. For example:

Mosquitoes relentlessly bit the Corps of Discovery members. (Subject: Mosquitoes, active verb: bit)

The chief of interpretation will present her budget to the superintendent. (Subject: chief of interpretation, active verb: will present)

Resource specialists conducted experiments to test the hypothesis. (Subject: specialists, active verb: conducted)

Passive Voice
The subject receives the action expressed in the verb. Notice that the subject and verbs change from the active voice examples above. For example:

The Corps of Discovery members were relentlessly bitten by the mosquitoes. (Subject: Corps of Discovery, verb: were bitten)

The budget will be presented to the superintendent by the chief of interpretation. (Subject: superintendent, verb: will be presented)

Experiments have been conducted to test the hypothesis by the resource specialists. (Subject: experiments, verb: have been conducted)

Detecting Passive Voice

You can recognize passive voice because the verb phrase will always include a form of *be, am, is, was, were, are,* or *been.* Another way to detect passive voice is that the sentence may include *by the* after the verb.

Changing Passive Voice to Active Voice

Overuse of passive voice can make your interpretive writing to seem flat and uninteresting. Sentences written in passive voice are generally longer and more complicated than sentences written in active voice. Interpretive writing is succinct. Challenge yourself to use an active voice in your interpretive writing. For example:

The brakes were slammed on by Brenda as the patrol cruiser sped downhill. (passive)

Brenda slammed on the brakes as the patrol cruiser sped downhill. (active)

Action on the annual budget is being considered by the committee. (passive)

The committee is considering action on the annual budget. (active)

The brochure is being read by most of the visitors. (passive)

Most of the visitors read the brochure. (active)

Active voice facilitates clear and concise sentences. Notice that the active sentences are shorter in all the examples where active voice sentences are compared to their passive voice counterparts. This also allows you to fulfill one of the rules for interpretive writers that must not be broken listed in Chapter 5, "Conventions and Rules for Interpretive Writers": Keep the writing short.

Active voice is forceful and authoritative. Consider this sign, which is written in passive voice. How would you rewrite it in active language?

ALLITERATION
AND POETRY

Alliteration and poetry are language forms that, because of their unique structures, help readers remember messages. Limit their use or they become trite. Used in moderation, they add interest to interpretive messages.

Alliteration is the repetition of the opening consonant sounds in words close to one another. Alliteration occurs in Old English poetry, medieval epics, and verse romances; it is common in modern-day children's books, newspaper headlines, and in tongue twisters.

Alliteration is enjoyable to read and fun to say. The purpose of alliteration in interpretive writing is to place stress on certain words. Notice the ideas emphasized by alliteration in Helen Keller's *The Seeing See Little*: "Touch each object you want to touch as if tomorrow your tactile sense would fail." Ms. Keller focuses on the t's in touch, to, tomorrow, and tactile to emphasize meaning.

This brief passage is from a film script titled "Running a River: The Wisconsin" by Sarah Minier Johnson.

> Four hundred-thirty miles the river stretches to the south and west, surrendering its waters to the Mississippi. Four hundred-thirty miles to the east and north, the river's source lies cold and silent.

The alliteration of *stretches, south,* and *surrendering* in the first sentence, as well as *source* and *silent* in the second sentence helps you remember the passages.

Another example of alliteration in interpretive writing comes from the first draft of the Wildlife Garden Way interpretive signs at the Oregon Zoo. Rex Ettlin offers this passage about the Kincaid's lupine.

> Kincaid's lupine (in the cages) needs upland prairie to survive. Urbanization and agriculture has replaced most upland prairies. The cages *protect* the *plants* from nibbling *peacocks*.

Here, the alliteration of *protect, plants,* and *peacocks* helps you remember the message about the need for caging the lupine resource.

The following are common examples of alliteration:

turn the tables
now or never
the more the merrier
super sonic
green as grass
hale and hearty
safe and sound
rubber baby buggy bumpers
julie jackson juggled the juicy, jiggly jello

An example of alliteration in poetry:

Small pond
Made by beavers
Swimming, jumping, fishing
Be still, relaxing, peaceful
Shining

The alliteration in poetry leads me to recall my first interpretive writing challenge. It was to create several labels for plants in a botanical conservatory. The reason for the project was to replace descriptive signs with labels that communicated the essence of the plants and the conservatory. The conservatory, built in 1903, housed subtropical plants, several planted at the time of construction. My goal was to make the conservatory and plants intellectually meaningful and connect the resource emotionally for the visitor. Obviously, there are several ways to accomplish that end; the one I chose was to interpret the resource through poetry. Poetry can provide emotional essence that is not possible with prose.

From literature such as Milton's *Paradise Lost,* I selected excerpts to make the intellectual/emotional connections. When I could not locate poems that fit my goal, I wrote them. I drew upon tanka, cinquain, haiku, and diamante styles to interpret individual plants and the conservatory. The product was interpretation that did not rely on facts, but on feelings evoked by the intellectual/emotional connections.

Two years later, planners relocated the conservatory and many of the plants for a new office building. The interpretive signs were lost during the move, so I do not have them to share. However, I can provide you the formulas for tanka, cinquain, haiku, and diamante styles of poetry, along with examples of each.

Tanka

A tanka is one of the earliest forms of Japanese poetry. From it, a variety of other forms began to emerge as early as the eighth century.

The basic form of a tanka is composed of five lines with 31 syllables in the pattern of 5-7-5-7-7. For example:

> Thawed, frozen water
> Rushing over rocks, past trees
> With force and with grace
> Carrying secrets and tales
> Of the life it left behind.

Cinquain

A cinquain is a five-line poetry form originating in France (*cinq* means five in French), pronounced *sin-kane*. Each line has a prescribed number of words or syllables. In a cinquain, line one contains one word that names an idea, a feeling, or a thing. Line two contains two words that describe it (what it looks like or feels like). Line three has three words that tell what it is doing, has done, or will do. Line four has a four-word phrase or four single words that tell how the author feels about it, an observation on it, or its effect on other things. Line five has one word that means the same as the word in line one, a synonym, or that refers to the title, that relates through connotation—a word to "sum it all up." For example:

> River
> Rapid, cold
> Cleansing speaking raging
> Bringing promise of renewal
> Lifeblood

Haiku

A haiku is a Japanese poetic form that developed from the tanka and became popular in the 16th century. It is an art of painting with words. One presents a picture, then isolates one part of it. By looking closely at the detail of the isolated fragment, more meaning is given to the whole.

There are three essential elements of haiku: The time is now; the place is here; the object brings us into direct contact with nature.

A haiku contains 17 syllables, usually in three lines, with a syllable pattern of 5-7-5. This example is composed by the Japanese poet Sekko:

> Fish in the river rise
> This peaceful summer day, and snap
> At little dragon-flies.

Diamante

A diamante is a poetry form in the shape of a diamond.

noun

adjective adjective

participle participle participle

noun noun noun noun

participle participle participle

adjective adjective

noun

Beginning and ending nouns are antonyms (opposites). In the center are four nouns related to both antonyms. This example of a diamante is written by my daughter Miranda:

Tree

Tall, green

Powerful, growing, beaming

Home, nest, axe, house

Falling, crying, crashing

Stump

Alliteration and poetry makes interpretive writing projects livelier when it is used sparingly. Like questions, both rhyming forms challenge the reader to focus deeper on the resource. The advantage of alliteration and poetry is that they have a lilt that targets the emotions and helps make connections with the intellect.

READABILITY INDEXES

At what reading level should interpretive messages be written? I have asked this of interpreters in my writing workshops. The highest frequency response is the eighth-grade level. When I ask why, the response I often get is that it is the lowest common reading level of the general public. And, to assure that the message reaches everyone, messages must be written at this level.

Many interpreters base their answer to the question on their perceived reading levels of popular print media. For instance, most declare that a *Time* magazine article selected at random has a higher reading level than a *People* magazine article. The examples beginning on page 92 illustrate that this notion may not be true. The real answer to the question, "At what reading level should interpretive messages be written?" is: It depends on your audience's characteristics.

I believe that in interpretation, the "general public" does not exist. What most interpretive writers consider the general public are in fact several publics, each with exclusive identifiable characteristics. Effective messages are written to meet the interests and needs of specific audiences. Specific public characteristic descriptions, such as age demographics and geographic distributions of audience members, appear in interpretive site plans. Writers familiar with the site plans are able to write interpretive messages that match their public's characteristics.

It may be that most of the readers/visitors have a high school education. Using readability measures facilitates writing specifically for them—or any audience. Readability indexes such as ones found in word processing programs like Microsoft Word, are powerful tools for interpretive writers. They measure the level of reading skills readers need in order to understand a given piece of writing. They are good predictors of the difficulty of documents. A numeric measure of the indexes is matched with grade levels. The grade levels are broken into parts of an academic year. It is possible to have a reading grade level of 3.5 or 10.1, for instance.

All readability measures apply a predetermined formula to the total number of words and the number of difficult words in the text. The Flesch-Kincaid reading ease score is calculated by applying a formula to the average number of words per sentence and the average number of syllables per word. The score will be from 0 to 100 with a score of 90–100 being very easy, 80–89 easy, 70–79 fairly easy, 60–69 standard, 50–59 fairly difficult, 30–49 difficult, and 0–29 very difficult.

How It Works

The Flesch-Kincaid Reading Ease score equals 206.835 minus (1.015 x Average Sentence Length) minus (84.6 x Average Syllables per Word.)

There are several readability measures, including: the Fog Index Coleman-Liau Grade Level, Bormuth Grade Level, and the Flesch-Kincaid Reading Ease scale. The Flesch-Kincaid scale is the program included in Microsoft Word software. Most interpretive writers I work with use Microsoft Word as their word processing program. Each time you use "Spelling and Grammar" under "Tools" on the toolbar, you can automatically get a readability assessment. To do this you need to reset the software to override its built-in default. Do this by selecting "Spelling and Grammar" from the "Tools" pull-down menu. Click the "Options" button and then check the "Show Readability Statistics" box under "Grammar." You will receive a Flesch-Kincaid readability table each time you ask the software to check spelling and grammar.

While reading indexes are valuable, it is unwise to rely on reading ease measures to predict readers' comprehension of concepts. Interpretive writers should consult various states' curriculum frameworks to determine what their audiences have learned in schools. Other resources like *The Dictionary of Cultural Literacy: What Every American Needs to Know* outline what adults should know by early adulthood.

Examples

The following are examples of grade level writing from different magazines. This illustrates that popular media do not follow a formula for a "general public."

"Remember Afghanistan?"
Time, March 8, 2004

> On this day in February, a driving blizzard has made Karzai's lair seem even more forbidding. Only one person gets through unchallenged: Zalmay Khalilzad, the U.S. ambassador to Afghanistan. Inside Karzai's office, the two men converse in English and Dari, one of Afghanistan's two official languages.

Flesch-Kincaid reading ease score 56.3, grade level 9.5.

"Fatal Reaction"
People, February 9, 2004

> Described by those who knew her as sweet and naive, Michelle appeared to have all the trappings of happiness—a sprawling home in the New Jersey suburbs, fancy cars, and three energetic young kids. Everything except a truly satisfying marriage.

Flesch-Kincaid reading ease score, 51.6, grade level 11.5.

"From Bad to Worse"
U.S. News and World Report, July 24, 2006

> At first, the Israelis tried nonlethal deterrence-diplomatic warnings, then sonic booms from fighter jets to remind the Gazans that Israel has the power to retaliate. Those failed. It was a sad demonstration of the truth in the metaphor that in the Middle East the law of nature prevails—an animal perceived as weak invites only attack.

Flesch-Kincaid reading ease score, 36.1, grade level 12.0.

"Hard Labor at Bear Gulch"
Natural History, July/August 2006

> Grumpy, fuzzy, scholarly type was beside himself. Halfway up the ten-foot-high rock wall he'd run out of toeholds, and he clung desperately to the tiny fingerholds above him. The wall was made of layers of shale, inch-thick ledges protruding irregularly from the mesa, and he couldn't find a higher one to stand on. The distinguished professor of physiology and evolution was stuck.

Flesch-Kincaid reading ease score, 58.3, grade level 9.1.

"A Sea is Born"
Wired, June 2006

> A new ocean is forming in the hottest place on Earth, and it's putting on one hell of a show. In the Afar Triangle—a region of northeastern Africa where summer temps hit 131 degrees Fahrenheit and scientists have armed bodyguards for protection against guerrillas—the ground is splitting apart, making room for a sea.

Flesch-Kincaid reading ease score, 51.8, grade level 10.6.

"How Not to Attract Tourists"
The Week, July 7-14, 2006, page16

> Manitoba's new motto "is, in a word, 'Lame-o,'" said John Gleeson in the *Winnipeg Sun*. The province handed over $600,000 to a marketing task force to come up with a new slogan to attract tourism, and in return we got this phrase: "Spirited energy." The first thing that struck me about the phrase is that it hardly rolls off the tongue. Try saying it three times fast and you just might choke to death.

Flesch-Kincaid reading ease score, 70.1, grade level 6.4.

The Flesch-Kincaid Reading Ease Score and Its Application to an Interpretive Text

The Flesh-Kincaid scale is applied to an interpretive text.

Brewer's Blackbird
Euphagus cyanocephalus

Blackbirds help us control plant-eating pests like caterpillars, beetles, and bugs. They also eat food scraps in parking lots.

Blackbirds travel in large flocks. Somehow, all the birds in the flock can change direction together, instantly, as if the flock were one giant bird.

When walking, this bird bobs its head forward in a jerky way. The male is black with yellow eyes. The female is grey with dark eyes.

© *Patricia McQuade, Earth Cards: Nature Trading Cards*

The Flesch-Kincaid reading ease score, 78.2, which translates to a grade level of 4.8. This grade level matches the demographic of the author's target audience.

WHAT TO AVOID

There are some things that interpretive writers should do and things that interpretive writer should avoid. It is important that writers be aware of, and follow the five elements of interpretive writing. It is also important that interpretive writers do everything possible to not confuse readers, to keep their messages short, simple, and goal directed for the audience they are writing for. In that vain, the following should be avoided: acronyms, initialisms, contractions, passé language, redundant wording, jargon, adverbs, and adjectives.

Private Language

Acronyms, initialisms, and contractions are forms of specialized "private" language that excludes audiences or slows reading ease. English is replete with these shortcuts, with organizations prone to inventing new language. The following story illustrates how an acronym hinders the communication process.

"BIMPO!" declared the $10,000-per-day consultant to the non-profit steering committee. "This is the acronym for all the attributes you should be looking for in recruiting board members." Emily leaned over to me and whispered, "What's a BIMPO?" Just as she asked, Roger continued, "I tried to fit the acronym to BINGO but couldn't make it work, so I came up with BIMPO instead." Eyebrows raised in bemused collective bewilderment. It appeared that his enthusiasm for shorthand communication was teetering on the absurd.

Roger attempted to formulate a meaningful acronym, knowing that acronyms are a common and useful form of communication in today's world. As a nationally renowned and well-traveled consultant, he knows that Americans enjoy using acronyms and initialisms. He understands that we live in an era of sound bites, entertainment news programs, jargon, e-mailing, and text messaging—living on the fast track of communication. What Roger does not understand is that the fast track of communication can be so esoteric that it becomes useless.

Like Roger, interpreters can become so enshrouded in their own professional jargon that they fail to communicate effectively. We frequently use acronyms, initialisms, and contractions without regard to whether our audiences know what the language shortcuts mean.

According the 15th edition of the *Chicago Manual of Style*, an acronym refers only to terms based on the initial letters of their various elements and read as single words (NATO, AIDS, CIG, and, of course, BIMPO). Initialisms refer to terms read as a series of letters (NAI, BLM, USACE). A contraction includes the first and last letters of the full word (Mr., Ph.D.). Acronyms and initialisms are the most commonly used in writing and speaking. They are jargon when audiences feel excluded.

Historians date the emergence of acronyms and initialisms to 63 B.C. in Rome when Marcus Tullius Tiro transcribed Roman Senate speeches using a form of shorthand that he devised. The shorthand notations consisted of numerous symbols and abbreviations. Little did he know that, one day, computer programmers and other professionals would develop entire dialects from his shorthand innovations.

I first became aware of the problems associated with acronyms and initializations becoming jargon when I worked with a group of nuclear engineers conducting teacher-training workshops for high school teachers. The sessions were replete with initialisms like NRC, EPA, and NEI. The teachers were confused and the presenters had to stop frequently to remind them that NRC referred to Nuclear Regulatory Commission, EPA meant Environmental Protection Agency, and NEI referred to the Nuclear Energy Institute. It occurred to me that the presenters felt comfortable using the initialisms that were their language. On the other hand, the audience members' ease of following the presentation was interrupted every time they had to remind themselves what initialisms like NRC, EPA, and NEI signified.

The engineers took for granted that their audience knew all of the engineers' commonly used acronyms and initialisms. This was a mistake. The engineers used language esoteric to their own profession and did not understand the characteristics of their audience.

I have experienced similar situations teaching undergraduates in natural resources programs. I assumed that all students understood the initialisms BLM, NPS, USDAFS, BIA, and USACE. Not true. Several times students would inquire what the letters stood for. It seemed logical to me that people aspiring for employment with the Bureau of Land Management would know what BLM meant. Not so.

We face a proliferation of short-cut communication. We are constantly introduced to new language to learn, such as, NRO (Natural Resource Officer), CTRS (Certified Therapeutic Recreation Specialist), and NIW (National Interpreters Workshop). I know you can list many others. Some are used so commonly that most of us have no idea what they stand for, like PDF (portable document format) and ZIP code (Zone Improvement Program). Others are ingrained in our culture and become versions of words changed beyond the original meaning; SPAM ("spiced ham") has been converted to mean junk mail. Heritage interpreters need to be aware of the terminology we use and make sure we are communicating in clear precise language to our audiences.

Roger was a well-paid consultant making a presentation to a steering committee seeking qualities to look for in potential board members for a non-profit museum. He invented an acronym to convey the attributes for the steering committee to remember. Unfortunately, the acronym did not make any sense. The acronym was memorable but did not convey a sensible message. As a member of the steering committee, I had to search my notes to recall that BIMPO meant "Brings enthusiasm, Interest, Money, Partnerships, Optimism." It is important that if you use shorthand language, you use language that makes sense.

Acronyms and initialisms are common shortcuts to written language that not everyone understands. The following story cautions that some of our language is outdated.

Passé Language: An Interpretive Story

Because their parents won a three-week Mediterranean cruise, Amy and Luke were given a treat. While their parents were away on the trip, Amy and Luke were staying with their grandmother who lived close to their home. It was always a festive holiday occasion when they visited her. This time was different. Nine and six years old respectively, they were going to continue to attend school, Luke at the elementary school a mile away, and Amy at the middle school around the corner.

The bed was extra-special-warm-and-cozy to Amy as she settled in for her first night's rest. She looked across the bedroom at Luke. He was already snuggled into bed gazing towards Amy with a big smile. He too, was excited to be at Grandmother's house.

At that moment, Grandmother opened the bedroom door. Bright yellow light from the hallway fixture pervaded the room, making the children squint as they looked towards Grandmother. "Oh, you are already in your beds!" she declared. "What wonderful children you are. Tomorrow is going to be a big day, so you will need your rest. I'll just tuck you in and kiss you both good night." She did as she said, and walked to the door. As she was leaving she turned and said, "Now remember Luke, you will have to be at the corner to catch the bus at eight o'clock." Luke indicated agreement with a reluctant nod. The bright yellow hallway light began to vanish as she continued to close the door, but before it was completely dark in the room she said good night once more and ended with, "Don't let the bedbugs bite!" The door clicked shut.

Amy sat up straight. Her eyes were fixed round and wide on the door. "Bedbugs?! Are there bugs in my bed, Luke?" she squealed. Luke was silent. "Luke, did you hear what Grandma said about bedbugs?"

"Grandma won't let them get you."

"Doesn't it worry you, Luke?"

"No. I'm worried about catching the bus. I'm afraid I won't run fast enough to catch it. Do you think the driver will slow down when he sees me?"

"Of course, silly, that's just a saying."

Luke thought for a long while. "Well, maybe the bedbugs thing is just a saying, too."

Can you sympathize with Amy and Luke? I am certain each of us has experienced an episode similar to theirs, probably with amusing consequences. Even as we grow older, we continue to encounter barriers to effective communication due to the language we select.

English is a complex language that confuses adults, too. More than 3,500 new words were added to the Oxford Dictionary in the last decade. It is impossible for us to know all the new words, let alone the old ones. However, using the language that our audiences are familiar with is critical in order for interpreters to communicate well. We need to be conscious that our audiences are increasingly varied geographically and ethnically and may not be accustomed to our preferred clichés, trite expressions, colloquialisms, jargon, idioms, and vernacularisms.

One of my friends in graduate school was Benny, a faculty member at Grambling University in Louisiana. Benny was on sabbatical leave from Grambling University, and was attending the same university as I. We were earning a similar degree. We had the same faculty advisor, Robert. Robert was health-conscious and every noon he went for a run on the university's track. One day, Benny and I were in Robert's office and Robert made the comment to Benny that he would like to run with him. Benny looked perplexed. When we left the office, Benny turned to me and said, "I don't want to go looking for ladies with him. Anyway, he's married." I explained that to Robert running did not imply meeting women; it meant the action of running. A relieved smile appeared on his face. He paused, then said, "I don't want to do that either."

Then again, some phrases like Grandmother's "bedbugs" have become ingrained in our culture because of common historical origins and should be kept as colorful language. It is up to us to determine which phrases work best with our diverse audiences.

Whereas some phrases are passé, others represent specialized language intended for specific professions or groups. Language used by an exclusive group or profession is meaningless to others. Each organization suffers the risk of inventing words and phrases not understood by their clients. Known as jargon, this pretentious language alienates readers.

During the 1980s, electrical generation companies were concerned about the growing demand for electricity. Pacific Gas and Electric (PG&E) in California responded with several programs designed to encourage conservation and inform the public that the company did not have the capital to invest in new power generation plants. Among the programs was an elementary school curriculum supplement for energy conservation. For three years, PG&E educators traveled the state offering workshops to teachers, showing them how to integrate the activities into their existing curricula. I observed four workshops.

Thirty or more teachers attended the workshops, with three PG&E presenters. The presenters were public relations personnel and were concerned that the teachers were unfamiliar with PG&E terminology. While two presenters conducted an activity, the third representative called out, "Jargon!" whenever she heard an energy provider word that the teachers might not understand.

The process was amusing at first, as the presenters were interrupted by a colleague, yelling "Jargon!" then telling the presenter the errant word and explaining the word usage to the audience. At first, the audience appreciated the explanations. Later, the audience reacted with annoyance as it became obvious that the industry has an exclusive language.

In the end, I found the interruptions instructive. They underscored that a profession develops its own metaphorical language not understood or used by others. Jargon is a shortcut to language that benefits the users, yet can be pretentious or meaningless to outsiders. It is shorthand for expressing ideas that are frequently discussed between members of a group, and can also have the effect of distinguishing those belonging to a group from those who do not.

Interpreters have their own language, using words the public is familiar with in other contexts. Some examples include:

"Visitors come to our sites to experience something new." (*Sites* is jargon.)

"Front-line interpreters provide the personal connection with the visitors."
(*Front-line* is jargon.)

"The theme of tonight's campfire talk is, 'Sacramento is indebted to Folsom Dam.'" (*Theme*, as used by interpreters may be considered jargon by audiences. Dictionaries define theme from the discipline of art, with the word topic as a synonym. Interpreters have chosen to use the word theme to express a deeper understanding of the word topic.)

What jargon-like terms do you and your colleagues use? Gene Ervine of the Alaska office of the Bureau of Land Management offers these examples of jargon: Tread Lightly! Leave No Trace! Ecosystem Management, Web of Life, Biodiversity, Watchable Wildlife, and Scenic Byway.

Redundant Wording

A challenge for writers is precision in the language we choose. Jargon, passé language, and private language present challenges difficult to overcome because they imbue or verbal communication style. Redundant wording, another challenge to clear writing comes from verbal communication.

The first thing to overcome is the impulse to write the same way we talk. Writing is more formal. Casual language is replete with redundant pairs. Eliminate the pairs in order to make the writing precise. Many pairs of words imply each other. For example, *finish* implies *complete*, so the phrase *completely finish* is redundant. Here are some common redundant pairs that I have seen in brochures and panels:

> past memories (all memories are of the past)
> terrible tragedy (aren't all tragedies terrible?)
> various differences (differences are various)
> end result (there are no beginning or middle results)
> each individual (each person is an individual)
> final outcome (outcomes are summative, therefore final)
> basic fundamentals (fundamentals are basic)
> free gift (by definition, gifts are supposed to be free)
> true facts (all facts are true)
> past history (history is about the past)
> important essentials (all essentials are important)
> unexpected surprise (surprise parties are intended to be unexpected)
> future plans (plans are about the future)
> sudden crisis (there are not planned crisis events)

Specific words imply their general categories, so we usually do not have to state both, such as:

> large in size (just use large)
> in a confused state (you would be in a state if you are confused)
> often times (just often)
> unusual in nature (unusual)
> of a bright color (bright)
> extreme in degree (extreme is sufficient)
> heavy in weight (heavy refers to weight)
> of an uncertain condition (uncertain)
> period of time (period implies time)
> honest in character (he is honest, we understand it is his character)
> round in shape (round is a shape)
> of cheap quality (if it's cheap it is of low quality)
> at an earlier time (earlier, tells all)

Wordiness

Interpretive writers sometimes use one or more extra words or phrases that seem to modify the meaning of a noun but do not add to the meaning of the sentence. These words or phrases can seem meaningful in the interpretive text, but are not. This wordiness is "filler" and needs removal.

Here is a list of words to eliminate in order to write concise sentences:

kind of	particular	really
sort of	definitely	individual
type of	actually	basically
specific	generally	for all intents and purposes

Some prepositional phrases are vague and should be replaced with simple words:

in order to (just use the word *to*)
a lot of (*many* works well)
in regard to (*about*)
at this time (*now* is what your are talking about)

Below are examples of wordy statements with associated concise rewrites:

During the 1960s, many car buyers preferred cars that were pink in color and shiny in appearance. (wordy)

During the 1960s, many car buyers preferred pink, shiny cars. (concise)

The microscope revealed a group of organisms that were round in shape and peculiar in nature. (wordy)

The microscope revealed a group of peculiar, round organisms. (concise)

Any particular type of interpretive talk is fine with her. (wordy)

Any interpretive talk is fine with her. (concise)

Collecting all the campground fees by 10 p.m. is an impossibility without some kind of extra help. (wordy)

Collecting all the campground fees by 10 p.m. is impossible without extra help. (concise)

For all intents and purposes, American industrial productivity in the 20th century generally depended on certain factors that are really more psychological in kind than of any given technological aspect. (wordy)

Twentieth-century American industrial productivity depended more on psychological than on technological factors. (concise)

Adverbs

Precision is vital in interpretive writing. Redundant wording, jargon, passé language, and adverbs make writing unclear. Adverbs are verbs or adjectives that end in "ly." An adverb can be unclear when it modifies a verb. Adverbs confuse readers who are seeking exacting interpretation. If the horse quickly galloped, just how fast did he gallop? Adverbs do not answer to what extent.

"I am dead to adverbs; they cannot excite me…. I cannot learn adverbs; and what is more I won't." This was Mark Twain's reply to a Boston girl in the June 1880 *Atlantic Monthly*.

William Zinsser points out in his fifth edition of *On Writing Well*, "Most adverbs are unnecessary. You will clutter your sentence and annoy the reader if you choose a verb that has a specific meaning and then add an adverb that carries the same meaning. Don't tell us that the radio blared loudly—'blare' connotes loudness. Don't write that someone clenched his teeth tightly—there's no other way to clench teeth. Again and again in careless writing, strong verbs are weakened by redundant adverbs."

Adverbs may sound appropriate, authentic, and trendy in spoken language. Writers use adverbs because they think they contribute emphasis, but often they do the reverse, because they are empty words, and they soften the meaning of a sentence.

Adverbs ending in "ly" distract from the action you are seeking to communicate in your interpretive writing. Eliminating adverbs requires work. It means searching for a good verb to give the sentence precise powerful meaning. Instead of "The bobcat watched steadily…" try, "The bobcat stared." An action verb creates a picture for the reader. The right action verb creates an enduring mental image. "Hurried" and "bolted" both imply quickness, but each creates its own image. With action verbs, you select the image you want to express, rather than letting the reader guess what you mean with an "ly" adverb.

Original: Actually, frowning angrily, she moved hurriedly towards him, saying very harshly, "You fool."

Revision: Scowling, she stalked towards him. "You fool."

Empty Words

actually, totally,

absolutely,

completely,

continually,

constantly,

continuously,

literally, really,

unfortunately,

ironically, incredibly,

hopefully, finally

Original: Sheila convincingly explains her position to Robert.

Revision: Sheila explains her position to Robert.

Original: The play carefully examines the disorder brought by civil war.

Revision: The play examines the disorder brought by civil war.

Adjectives

I am sure that many of you, upon reading the first paragraph of this chapter, turned to this page and asked, "What's wrong with adjectives? Why avoid them? Adjectives make my interpretive writing colorful." The issue is that many interpretive writers overuse adjectives. They rely on adjectives to provide meaning when they should be looking for better nouns.

In William Strunk and E.B. White's *The Elements of Style*, rule number 17 in a chapter titled "Principles of Composition" is "Omit needless words." Most adjectives are needless. William Zinsser states in the sixth edition of *On Writing Well*, "Like adverbs, [adjectives] are sprinkled into sentences by writers who don't stop to think that the concept is already in the noun." The reader knows that dirt is brown and daffodils are yellow. Writing "the brown dirt" or "the yellow daffodils" adds unnecessary words to your text.

On the other hand, when selected with care, adjectives provide color to writing. Mark Twain stated, "When you catch an adjective, kill it. No, I don't mean utterly, but kill most of them—then the rest will be valuable. They weaken when they are close together. They give strength when they are wide apart. An adjective habit…, once fastened upon a person, is as hard to get rid of as any other vice."

When a writer eliminates the habits that I addressed above, his or her message can be powerful, as the following passage illustrates. The text is a panel in the "Our Peoples" exhibition of the National Museum of the American Indian in Washington, DC. I have included the following text by Paul Chaat Smith to highlight how writing can be economical and powerful. The text is a mere 143 words, yet it conveys a gripping story. The narrative is broken into three paragraphs for easy reading. Each paragraph averages but four sentences. The sentences are easy to comprehend because they average only 12 words. There are no passive sentences, instead favoring active sentences comprising strong action verbs. Mr. Smith eschews acronyms, contractions, redundancies, jargon, passé language, vernaculars, and adverbs. He uses few adjectives and selects phrases like "kingdom of death" for emotional impact. The reading level is ninth grade.

Infinite Thousands

Contact withered the indigenous people of the Americas. With little immunity to European diseases, Native people fell victim to smallpox, measles, influenza, mumps, and other diseases. From 1492 to 1650, contagions claimed as many as nine lives out of ten.

The kingdom of death extended from Chile to New England. There, in 1616, a wave of disease swept in ahead of the Mayflower's Pilgrims. By the time the ship landed, the plagues had emptied entire Indian villages. Cold and hungry Pilgrims dug up graves and ransacked abandoned houses in search of buried corn. In December 1620, the colonists settled in a deserted Indian Village. They named it Plymouth.

The epidemics raged for 150 years. The biological catastrophe was unprecedented in human history: an extinction event that spanned continents. Sorrow and heartbreak cloaked a shattered world that in 10,000 years had never faced such disaster.

Tangible(s): Native people, Americas, smallpox, measles, influenza, mumps, Pilgrims, Plymouth, Indian Village, abandoned houses, buried corn, 10,000 years

Intangible(s): kingdom of death, wave of disease, epidemics raged, extinction event, shattered world

Universal(s): disease, extinction, history, sorrow, disaster, death, immunity

Emotional/Intellectual Connection: The text gives information attached to emotion. The reader, by virtue of his race, places value on the connection.

Stewardship Component: none explicit in the text

Does the writing encourage the reader to want to learn more? Yes, in this introductory panel to the exhibit, the reader is inspired to go after the rest of the story.

PART THREE

final steps

THE CHALLENGE OF INTERPRETIVE WRITING

Natural and cultural heritage interpretation methodology is organized according to a personal communication ideal that regards the most effective interaction as between a well-skilled, knowledgeable, passionate interpreter and a motivated visitor. This framework facilitates the implementation of the principle elements of interpretation.

From their own perspectives, John Muir, Enos Mills, and Freeman Tilden each discussed the best ways to communicate verbally with motivated audiences. Their concerns were how to best communicate with audiences of one person to audiences of hundreds of visitors.

When the audience is more than one visitor, the desire is for the interpreter to use techniques that make everyone feel as though it is a one-to-one interaction. Interpretation is most effective when it follows this one-to-one communication model.

Today, there are a limited number of trained front-line interpreters to fulfill this ideal. Consequently, emphasis is on communicating messages through non-personal approaches. Managers realize that the cost-per-visitor contact of brochures, signage, and Web sites is less than the cost of personal interpretation contact. Non-personal techniques have the potential of reaching larger audiences than front-line messages.

Non-personal interpretation can be used when an interpreter is not available, but should never replace an interpreter when first-person interpretation is more appropriate. The challenge of non-personal interpretation is to match the potential effectiveness of one-to-one personal interpretation. Interpretive writers apply their skills and established principles to accomplish this ambition.

A Challenge to Interpretive Writers

Interpretive messages support goals, whether the goals relate to persuasive articles about global warming or a museum label about a 19th-century loom. These goals appear in two categories: management and educational. These two categories often overlap, as some goals demand both categories. Management goals include law enforcement messages, resource protection messages, and site-specific logistical messages. Law enforcement messages outline appropriate behavior and often include the consequences of violating behavior guidelines. Resource protection messages explain a resource and how to maintain its integrity. Resource-based, site-specific logistical messages state how to interact with the resource to your benefit. Of the three, management-related law enforcement messages are the most difficult to write with interpretive elements.

Managers often want brusque messages that rebuff undesirable behavior. The messages include words or phrases like, *no, not,* and *do not,* or direct warnings. Although interpretive texts can have negative words, I believe it is important to avoid them. Words that connote negativism express disapproval of projected behavior, whether the projection is accurate or not. The following example has an added air of superiority by calling an airport an "Air Operations Area." How would you write a sign that dissuades people from entering a restricted area without using negative words?

On the other hand, the next example of a management message gives a positive impression. Visitors receive the flyer at the entrance stations as they enter Yellowstone National Park. Notice the strong visual impact of color, and graphics. Also, see how the writer made use of phrases rather than complete sentences. The combination of graphic design and grammar almost assures that anyone who sees the handout will read it.

Positive behavioral messages will include why a desired behavior is important to the resource and to the reader. In the example above, that message is explicit for the reader and implicit for the resource. The only change I would make to this flyer is to replace "DO NOT APPROACH BUFFALO" with a phrase like, "It is hazardous to approach buffalo."

Resource protection messages often have negative words, too. The best messages omit them and focus on extolling the assets of the resource to the reader. Every site has a purpose for its existence. Museums archive and preserve artifacts, historic dwellings tell a story about people and events, parks conserve natural resources. Managers often see the need to introduce messages that they feel visitors must have in order to understand and enjoy the resource. What program-supportive messages must you give your readers?

The following text is from a panel located on a trail at Devil's Orchard in Craters of the Moon National Monument and Preserve. It is written by David Clark at Harpers Ferry Center with contributions from Mary Lou Herlihy. The purpose of Devil's Orchard trail is to communicate a resource management message.

Walking Softly

Left alone, the volcanic rock of Devil's Orchard will slowly break down. The actions of visitors, though, have hurried this process, and partly destroyed a scene of beauty.

At this spot, visitors have broken the surface of this lava flow by walking on top of it. Their weight has crushed the cinder soil and formed a path to the small "cave."

By congressional mandate, park managers must protect these exceptional volcanic features, as well as make them enjoyable for visitors. When "protection" and "enjoyment" seem at odds, which of them do we choose? When enthusiasm today ruins a resources for tomorrow, how do we know what to do?

The third management-related message is the site-specific logistical text. These messages are descriptive as well as prescriptive. They help the reader understand how to interact with the site and how to process what they experience. The example below is from Holly Reed of Wildways Illustrated of Los Gatos, California. Notice how the text first describes the slough and its *importance*, then advises how the reader can best experience the resource.

Critical Resource, Natural Beauty
Watsonville Slough's "Last Mile"

This waterway is the critical last mile of the Watsonville Slough as it joins the Pajaro River and empties into Monterey Bay. These wetlands provide flood protection by storing storm run-off, act as a filtration system, and replenish groundwater.

This is important habitat and breeding grounds for many species of fish and varieties of wildlife. The diverse native plant community provides food and nesting places, as well as erosion control along the banks and mudflats.

Stop for a moment to observe the beauty. Light reflects off the water as it flows to the Pajaro. The snowy egret artfully stalks its meal. The pied-billed grebe swims, jerking its head quickly to and fro. If you disturb it, the great blue heron will take to the air, issuing a gravelly protest. The longer you quietly sit, the more you will see and hear.

The other interpretive message goal category is educational. The traditional way of approaching this is answering the question, "What program-supportive messages *do you want* to give your readers?" I believe a better way to approach writing the message is from the orientation of the reader, "What messages *do your readers want?*" This orientation accepts that the reader has self-identified an interest in the theme and has placed himself in the position to be receptive to the message. This orientation requires that you know your audience characteristics and that you can anticipate what they are looking for. Readers want to know, "What is the story of this place/resource?" "What does it mean to me?" and "How can this experience make my life better?"

The following sign from Waterton Lakes National Park in Alberta, Canada, illustrates interpretation that acknowledges what visitors want to know about the site.

Most educational interpretive messages are written for people looking to fulfill what psychologist Abraham Maslow termed "growth needs." Having met physiological, safety, security, social, and esteem needs, most interpretive audiences

are seeking knowledge for many reasons. These might include knowledge for its own sake, for inspiration, life-long learning opportunities, appreciation of unfamiliar cultures, and pro-social stewardship messages. The intent of most educational interpretive writing is to address these personal growth needs.

Julie Clark of the Bureau of Land Management in California contributes the following panel located near the entrance of the Headwaters Forest. This area was private until purchased for public use after a decade-long campaign by several government and conservation groups to acquire and then preserve this old-growth redwood forest. Now that it is open to the public, visitors are highly motivated to experience this area. This sign, one of the panels along the Elk River Trail, helps visitors understand who once lived there.

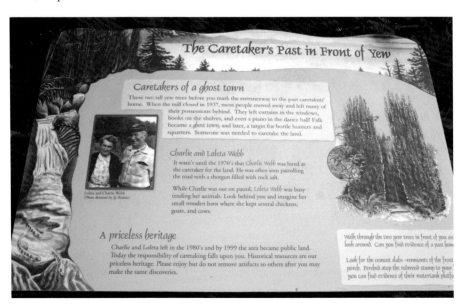

Whether the goal of your writing is educational or managerial, your challenge is to write so that the reader feels you are talking with them. Do this by knowing your audience's characteristics and the intangible perceptions that apply to your resource.

ASSESSING INTERPRETIVE WRITING ELEMENTS

Good writing exhibits several characteristics including its relevance to the reader, carrying a thematic message, accomplishing a goal, correct grammar, and clear structure. Writing that is thematic, goal-directed, and structurally and grammatically correct is often only informative. Interpretive writing, as a genre, inspires readers to make emotional and intellectual connections and to care about the subject, whether it is a relic, object, resource, or concept.

I have heard the frustration of interpretive writers who feel they cannot get good responses from colleagues or supervisors regarding the quality of their writing. "My supervisor handed my copy back and said, 'It looks good to me.'" Or, "I gave the text to some colleagues to read, and they made come grammatical changes, and said the content looks alright. What I want to know is *is it interpretive?*"

I have heard these comments enough to want to do something about it: to apply the elements of interpretive writing to a measurement instrument. The measurement instrument would provide the common language and criteria by which supervisors and colleagues can assess any writing for interpretive elements.

The following is a list of criteria for you to use in order to evaluate your writing. Six hundred fifty-five interpreters from the private sector and several government agencies have used these criteria to review more than 2,000 writing samples. Their anecdotal and written feedback regarding the utility of these criteria have demonstrated to me that the criteria—when used in an assessment form—provides evaluation of the writing and direction for improvement.

Interpretive Writing Criteria

- The writing identifies tangibles.

- The writing provides an opportunity for the reader to form an emotional connection with the subject (an artifact, resource, object, relic, concept).

- The writing reveals the way to make intellectual connections to the subject.

- The writing relates to the life of the reader.

- The writing provokes the reader to think, do, and/or feel something new.

- The writing connects universal concepts to the tangible attributes of the subject.

- The writing encourages the reader to care about the subject.

- The writing facilitates a connection between the interests of the reader and the inherent meanings of the subject.

- The writing addresses a complete storyline.

As I stated earlier, *each* wayside panel, museum label, or Web page does not have to include all five of these elements of interpretive writing. Also, each panel, label, or Web page does not have to contain all the above criteria. However, the *project as a whole* must have all five elements, and demonstrate all the criteria to be interpretive.

Interpretive Writing Assessment Forms

I suggest that a minimum of three reviewers receive a form to evaluate the content of a text for its interpretive elements. The advantage of this process is that the writer and the reviewers are using the same criteria for measuring the degree of interpretive elements present in the copy. The multiple review process gives the writer feedback regarding the strengths and weakness of his or her text. The assessment process also encourages a dialogue between the writer and the reviewers.

A Likert-type scale is included with the assessment criteria. I have found that some writers want a numeric evaluation of their writing. It is not critical to use the numeric scale. It is critical to make comments, however. I have found that writers want critiques from their colleagues. The area for comments provides space for acknowledging strengths in the writing and recommendations for improving the writing.

It is important to fill in every blank space when serving as a reviewer. The process of filling in a blank space encourages deeper consideration, and information that is more useful for the writer.

Interpretive Writing Assessment Form A

Writer   Reviewer

Title of Sample

1. The writing identifies tangibles.

           1   2   3   4   5   6   7
    not identified   well identified

Comments – strengths and recommendations for improvement:

2. The writing provides the opportunity for the reader to form an emotional connection with the subject.

           1   2   3   4   5   6   7
    not provided   well provided

Comments – strengths and recommendations for improvement:

3. The writing reveals a way to make intellectual connections to the subject.

           1   2   3   4   5   6   7
    not revealed   well revealed

Comments – strengths and recommendations for improvement:

Interpretive Writing Assessment Form B

Writer   Reviewer

Title of Sample

1. The writing relates to the life of the reader.

        1   2   3   4   5   6   7
    not related   well related

Comments – strengths and recommendations for improvement:

2. The writing provokes the reader to think, do, and/or feel something new.

        1   2   3   4   5   6   7
    does not provoke   strong provocation

Comments – strengths and recommendations for improvement:

3. The writing connects universal concepts to the tangible attributes of the subject.

        1   2   3   4   5   6   7
    not connected   well connected

Comments – strengths and recommendations for improvement:

Interpretive Writing Assessment Form C

Writer   Reviewer

Title of Sample

1. The writing encourages the reader to care about the subject.

            1   2   3   4   5   6   7

no encouragement   strong encouragement

Comments – strengths and recommendations for improvement:

2. The writing facilitates a connection between the interests of the reader and the inherent meanings of the subject.

            1   2   3   4   5   6   7

no connection   strong connection

Comments – strengths and recommendations for improvement:

3. The writing addresses a whole storyline.

            1   2   3   4   5   6   7

no storyline   connected storyline

Comments – strengths and recommendations for improvement:

THE EDITING PROCESS

Editing is not proofreading. Editing is removing every word that is unclear, confusing, or redundant. Editing is replacing dull words with rich language—a marriage of action verbs and emotive words. Editing is making a passage concise and assuring that every word is needed to meet the goal of the text. It is no secret that many major books and articles are edited down to less than half their original size. Editing is the process of taking a text and making it engaging without losing any meaning. I have chosen to divide the process into two exclusive methods: editing for content and editing for clarity.

Editing for Content

Does the text relate to an interpretive plan, goal, or objective? Does the text meet the needs of the audience or the site for which it is written? Look for sentences that best answer these questions so that you can identify a logical progression.

Fact-checking is critical to identifying untrue information used in interpretive texts. Access Web sites like snopes.com, purportal.com, and hoaxbusters.ciac.org, to see if the information you are using is part of an unsubstantiated urban myth.

When using historical data or science research data, give the text to colleagues who are expert in the discipline for their evaluation of the data's accuracy. If colleagues are unavailable, hire a freelance fact-checker. The checker will make sure that all figures and numbers match their references in the text and that they are accurate. A fact-checker will also collect approval on quotes, dates, names, agencies, statistics, citations, and other represented facts. Contact the editors of popular magazines in the discipline you are writing about for recommendations of freelance fact-checkers.

I received a hard copy of the following several years ago from a friend when I was teaching science classes at a university. My friend felt that the story would be a compelling supplement to my classes, as it relates how societal imperative affects science. I agreed. I never used the handout, but kept it filed just in case. Since he sent it to me in 1993, I have seen it with minor alterations on seven Internet sites.

The story is accurate according to each site.

"History of the Rail Gauge"
The U.S. Standard railroad gauge (distance between the rails) is 4 feet, 8.5 inches. Why was that gauge used? Because that is the way they built them in England, and English expatriates built the U.S. railroads. Why did the English people build them like that? Because they are the same people who built the pre-railroad tramways, and that is the gauge they used to build the first rail lines. Why did "they" use that gauge then? Because the people who built the tramways used the same jigs and tools that they used for building wagons, which used that wheel spacing. Why did the wagons use that odd wheel spacing? Well, if they tried to use any other spacing the wagons would break on some of the old, long-distance roads, because that is the spacing of the old wheel ruts. So, who built these old rutted roads? The first long-distance roads in Europe were built by Imperial Rome for the benefit of their legions. The roads have been used ever since. And the ruts? Roman war chariots first made the initial ruts, which everyone else had to match for fear of destroying their wagons. Since the chariots were made for or by Imperial Rome, they were alike in the matter of wheel spacing. Thus, the United States standard railroad gauge of 4 feet, 8.5 inches derives from the original specification for an Imperial Roman army war chariot. Specs and bureaucracies live forever.

I came across the hard copy of the story in my file cabinet when seeking inspiration for an editorial in *The Interpreter* magazine. After re-reading it I thought it must be true; after all, I have seen it in much the same form since 1993. Nonetheless, I decided to fact-check it before using it as a lead for an editorial. I am glad that I did.

The story does not qualify as a myth according to snopes.com and purportal.com, but it does contain inaccuracies. I think that the imprecision comes from the desire to keep the story short. This leads to false cause-effect relationships. For instance, only some English expatriates built U.S. railroads, there were many other nationalities involved, and there is no evidence that English expatriates influenced the gauge that was used. According to snopes.com, the story asserts several more linkages that are unproven.

It is important to fact-check stories and their sources. I have a network of authorities, and a list of Web sites to assist me in researching topics. I rely mostly on knowledgeable people, but Web sites that debunk are good resources in the early stages of projects. I was looking for inspiration for an editorial and I found the History of the Rail Gauge. I learned that the facts of the story are suspect, and I dropped the project.

Editing for Clarity
Identify the theme and sub-themes of the interpretive text. Check to see if the

central idea of each paragraph relates to the theme or to a sub-theme. Find the central idea of each paragraph and reduce it to a word or phrase. List the paragraph ideas; make sure they are a logical progression leading to answering the "So what?" of your theme.

Now, consider each paragraph at random. Examine only the information in that paragraph, and not how it relates to the whole text. Does the text offer enough details in the paragraph to support that word or idea? Decide whether all details are relevant. Delete any details and words that do not target the idea or phrase.

Look at the text in its entirety. Does each paragraph relate to the previous and follow in a logical progression? Notice whether you have clear transitions between paragraphs. If not, add new ones or rearrange your paragraphs to make the transitions smoother.

Review the text for the following pronouns: *it, this, they, their,* and *them.* Identify the noun that the pronoun replaces. If you cannot find a noun, insert one beforehand or change the pronoun to a noun. If you can find a noun, be sure it agrees in number and person with your pronoun.

Look for words that provide parallel structures: *such as, and, or, not only, but also, either, or, neither, nor,* and *both.* Make sure that the items connected by these words are in the same grammatical form.

Examine the text for the conjunctions: *and, but, for, or, nor, so,* and *yet.* Consider if there is a complete sentence on each side of the conjunction. If so, place a comma before the conjunction. Now, skim the paper, stopping at every comma. If there is a complete sentence on each side of the comma, add a conjunction after the comma or replace the comma with a semicolon.

Look for words ending in "ly." They are either adverbs or adjectives. Rid them from your sentences with action verbs and enlivened syntax.

Hunt for meaningless words. Writers often have a preconception of how many words they want to write, which results in padding with words that mean nothing. Replace them with emotive words like *power, feel, strength, hope,* or whatever fits the mood of the piece.

Search for fillers: *like, of its, and so it, that, well, sometimes, some of the time, perhaps, quite possibly,* or similar phrases. Erase them!

Proofreading

Harry MacAnarney was one of my academic advisors at Kansas State University. His field of expertise was the biological sciences. Yet, Harry had an interesting hobby outside the sciences, proofreading. On several occasions when I went to his office for a conference, I would find him engrossed in proofing and correcting news magazines. There on his desk were open copies of the most recent issues of *Time, Newsweek,* and *U.S. News and World Report.* Sprinkled on the pages were red ink marks noting semicolons in the place of commas, periods instead of dashes, and whole sentences crossed out. Harry was a stickler.

Proofreading is a craft and an art. You can learn the elemental aspects of proofreading, but there are some people, like Harry, who just seem to have a knack. I thought that learning the elemental aspects was enough. I learned the truth after I began editing and proofing *The Interpreter* for the Western Interpreters Association. I had help from at least six other people. Nevertheless, after each issue was mailed, I would find at least one typographic error. It was only after I found a proofreader that had artful talent like Harry that the magazines no longer had typographical and punctuation errors.

Here is my suggestion: find a proofreader who sees it as an art, someone who has fun proofreading, and "put them on your payroll." Nurturing a close relationship with a good proofreader does not preclude you proofing your own text, though. Here are my recommendations for proofreading for those of us who do not have the knack. Take breaks. Even five-minute breaks will help clear your head and allow you more productivity. The purpose is to read with a fresh mind.

Slow is the operative word. If you read at a normal speed, you will not give yourself time to spot errors. Apply the following steps to finding mistakes.

1. Use your computer spell checker and grammar checker.
2. Print it out and read it.
3. Point out each word with your finger as you read.
4. Read your copy backwards to focus on spelling.
5. Look at your text upside-down for typographic errors.
6. Give it to a colleague or friend to read. Choose someone who understands the audience and the goal of the text.
7. Read your text out loud and also silently. Do not look for any particular mistake, such as missing spaces, font sizes, or consistency. Keep an open mind.
8. Read holding a blank sheet of paper under each line of text. This encourages you to make a line-by-line review of the text.
9. Proof the text to make sure the headings agree.
10. Double-check the accuracy of italic, bold, or otherwise different fonts.

The final stages of the writing process include editing and proofreading. The technology of grammar and spell checking has made editing and proofing easier, but it brings danger, too. Word processors make this stage of the process more critical. Word processors allow writers to move words, phrases, sentences, and paragraphs with ease. Too often, this results in leaving behind and undetected confusing incomplete sentences and paragraphs. Effective editing and proofreading mitigates these hazards.

20

CONCLUSION

I want to reiterate the first purpose of this book as I outlined in the introduction. My belief is that interpretive writing is a genre with elements that are identifiable and measurable.

The framework I offered in "Assessing Interpretive Writing Elements" serves three functions. The first function is a reminder to help you shape your text to meet the criteria. The second function is to stimulate dialog between you, the writer, and those assessing the degree to which your writing is interpretive based on the elements. Finally, the framework provides a common language shared by you, the project manager, and text reviewers.

The assessment framework is a guideline. The guideline is not a rigid prescription to which all interpretive writing must conform. Indeed, even using the framework, there are myriad ways to write an interpretive text. It depends on the talent of the writer. Several state and federal agencies have established style manuals by which all writers must conform; this is not the intent of the framework and assessment criteria I present. Interpreters in the National Park Service and many members of the National Association for Interpretation, however, recognize the criteria as basic elements of interpretation and of interpretive writing. There are other aspects of good writing aside from the five elements. I feel these are the most important.

When I began this project, I solicited contributions from 345 writers and front-line interpreters. I received many. Along with the contributions there were suggestions included about the possible content of this book. Several people offered what they feel are the characteristics of interpretive writing. Some of those characteristics are that interpretive writing is enjoyable, personable, relevant, creative, purposeful, humorous, organized, thematic, and informative. All of these are credible descriptors of interpretive writing, and I believe I have acknowledged each. However, I chose not to use them in the framework and in the resulting assessment forms, because the five criteria are easier to assess and provide more effective feedback to the writer.

It is my hope that you use the framework of the five elements of interpretive writing, along with your writing talent, to author messages that are enjoyable, personable, creative, light-hearted, and informative. Moreover, I hope that you always keep in mind the fundamental precept of interpretation to honor the curiosity of your audience.

APPENDIX:
SELECTED RESOURCES

Beck, Larry, and Ted Cable. *Interpretation for the 21st Century*. Sagamore Publishing: Champaign, IL. 1998.

Brochu, Lisa. *Interpretive Planning*. InterpPress: Fort Collins, CO. 2003.

Brochu, Lisa, and Tim Merriman. *Personal Interpretation: Connecting Your Audience to Heritage Resources*. InterpPress: Fort Collins, CO. 2002.

Carson, Rachel. *The Sense of Wonder*. Harper Row: New York. 1956.

Hale, Constance. *Sin and Syntax*. Broadway Books: New York. 1999.

Ham, Sam. *Environmental Interpretation*. North American Press, Fulcrum Publishing: Golden, CO. 1992.

Harris, Robert. *When Good People Write Bad Sentences*. St. Martin's Griffin: New York. 2004.

Heintzman, James. *Making the Right Connections: A Guide for Nature Writers*. University of Wisconsin-Stevens Point. 2006.

King, Stephen. *On Writing*. Pocket Books: New York. 2000.

Leopold, Aldo. *A Sand County Almanac*. Oxford University Press: New York. 1949.

Lewis, William J. *Interpreting for Park Visitors*. Eastern Acorn Press: Philadelphia, PA. 1989.

Longknife, Ann. *The Art of Styling Sentences*. Barron's, Hauppauge: New York. 2002.

O'Conner, Patricia. *Woe Is I*. Riverhead Books: New York. 1996.

Serrell, Beverly. *Exhibit Labels: An Interpretive Approach*. AltaMira Press: Walnut Creek. 1996.

Strunk, William, and E.B. White. *The Elements of Style*. Macmillan: New York. 1979.

Tilden, Freeman. *Interpreting Our Heritage*. Chapel Hill, NC. 1957.

Veverka, John. *Interpretive Master Planning*. Acorn Naturalists: Tustin, CA. 1998.

Zinsser, William. *On Writing Well*. Collins Publishing: New York. 2001.

APPENDIX:
CONTRIBUTORS

Deirdre Ballou, San Diego Zoo, California
Larry Beck, San Diego State University, California
Virginia D. Bourdeau, Oregon State University 4-H Specialist, Oregon
Judy Fort Brenneman, Greenfire Creative, Fort Collins, Colorado
Julie Clark, Bureau of Land Management, Arcata, California
Heather Currey, Oregon State Parks, Port Orford, Oregon
Denise Dahn, Dahn Design, Seattle, Washington
Caryn Davidson, Joshua Tree National Park, California
Barb DeChristopher, Custom Direct, Roselle, Illinois
Deanna DeChristopher, Freelance writer, Chicago, Illinois
Linda Duvanich, Arcata, California
Jenny Dyer, ECOS Communications, Denver, Colorado
Cyndi Eide, Bureau of Land Management, Billings, Montana
Erin Engelman, Custom Direct, Roselle, Illinois
Emily Evans, Bureau of Land Management, Arcata, California
Gene Ervine, Bureau of Land Management, Alaska Office
Faye Goolrick, Interpretive Writer, Atlanta, Georgia
Charis Henrie, Oregon Zoo, Portland, Oregon
Sarah Minier Johnson, Owner, Backporch Media Production, Philomath, Oregon
Mary Lou Herlihy, National Park Service, Oakland, California
Jon Kohl, Interpretive Writer and Planner, Costa Rica
Miranda Leftridge, Swan Valley, Montana
Betsy A. Leonard, Environmental Educator, Parachute, Colorado
Patricia McQuade, Earth Cards: Nature Trading Cards, Watsonville, California
Larry Mink, Idaho State Parks, Coeur d'Alene, Idaho
Kelly Mulvihill, Janet Huckabee Arkansas River Valley Nature Center, Arkansas
Denise Newman, Redwood Community Action Agency, Eureka, California
Stephen Packard, Chicago Wilderness, Illinois
Holly Reed, Wildways Illustrated, Los Gatos, California

Deborah Richie Oberbillig, Deborah Richie Communications, Missoula, Montana
Beverly Slavens, Ouachita Baptist University, Arkadelphia, Arkansas
Billy Strasser, Klondike Gold Rush National Historical Park, Alaska
Russell Virgilio, Lassen Volcanic National Park, California
Anne Warner, Oregon Zoo, Portland, Oregon

INDEX